# Kitchen Gangster?

The Story of a Serial Entrepreneur

*An Investigation by John Newton*

First published in the United Kingdom by Next Century Books
September 2009
Second Print - September 2010

An imprint of
Complete Access Films Limited
Wing
Bedfordshire
LU7 0NW

Cover Design & Layout by Jay Purcell
Cover Photograph by John Carey / www.john-carey.com

A CIP catalogue Record for this title is available from the British Library

ISBN 978 0 9544011 9 1

First published by Next Century Books February 2010
Reprinted September 2010

*To Vance Miller*
*without whom I'd have nothing to write about*

## *The Author*

**John Newton** was born in London and educated in Germany before serving in Kenya with the armed forces and the Kenya Police.

After leaving the Kenya Police he stayed on as a businessman and travelled widely throughout Africa, Arabia and India. He speaks German and Swahili. He broadcast extensively on Kenya and Uganda Radio, writing and producing his own programmes and wrote of his travels in a London newspaper. He has one surviving son, a successful businessman who lives in Sussex with his wife and four children.

John Newton lives in Bedfordshire with his wife, Pam, and writes full time.

Other Work By John Newton
**WHITE SUNRISE.**
The first of an East African Trilogy

### *Acknowledgements*

I worked hard on this book but so did others to whom I owe a debt of gratitude. Barry Cooper worked for almost a year on meticulous research, digging up all sorts of facts and incidents that he presented in a clear and detailed fashion making my task of gathering together and writing this complex story a great deal easier. And Tim Purcell, a talented film-maker, writer and editor whose skill at filleting my text and designing layouts added enormously to my small talent. And all those who agreed to be interviewed at The Mill, at newspaper offices, at Trading Standards in Oldham who gave me a gracious welcome and others in odd places such as pubs, my motor car or out on the pavement. And Vance Miller for all the time and patience he gave over a year and a half of persistent enquiry into his personal affairs and life.

### *Author's Note*

This book is written as fact using mainly the words of those interviewed. The only changes are where spoken word translates awkwardly to written word. So in some places I modified speech sequence or added or subtracted a few words to ease flow of diction. Nowhere is sense or meaning of a word or phrase changed to distort a point and all Interviews are available for anyone who wishes to check. I have also cut out most of the swearing that Vance uses as speech punctuation since, while it detracted nothing from the story, it also added nothing and would certainly have been offensive to many in written form.

*John Newton*

### *No Disclaimer*

This book is written around ninety-eight percent directly in the spoken words of those interviewed. I made only a few minor adjustments where speech pattern or idiom did not translate to the written page. The adjustments do not affect the meaning or sense of what was spoken into my digital recorder. I also cut out a lot of swearing.

In preparing and writing this story I took a completely neutral standpoint, avoiding hints of support for either side or offering my opinion on what was said in so many interviews. That remains the case. All and any opinions in this book are those of the person being interviewed and not mine.

Since every person in the book is real I see no need for the usual weasel-word disclaimer that all characters are my invention. They are all a product of their own imagination and require no embellishment from me.

## *Chronology*

This book is not written in precise time sequence. The nature of many interviews meant that they swapped, overlapped or repeated what the interviewee or others said. So I wrote chronology of Chapters in what seemed best to tell a complex tale as logically as possible. Any resulting confusion is my fault and I accept all blame.

# Prologue

At dawn on a freezing 29th November 2006, one hundred and thirty Police and Trading Standards officers smashed into Maple Mill in Oldham and four houses in Rochdale and other nearby towns. With press and television pre-warned and crowding close to film, photograph and report, news of the whole action spread across local and national media in blasting headlines and excited prose.

This unprecedented and aggressive Raid by such a force might be seen as cracking an international terrorist cell; a big drugs bust or lethal arms raid in some hell's kitchen.

No. The Raids took place on ordinary commercial premises and simple homes in a search for evidence of fraud. Fraud! The raid netted an enormous amount of paperwork along with computers, telephones and hard discs.

Despite the size, aggression and drama of the Raid only four arrests were made and the excitement died because nothing happened for almost six months when charges of conspiracy to defraud were brought against Vance Miller, the main target, and three of his senior staff.

A further two-and-a-half years passed before the case finally reached court in September 2009. During that time the Maple Mill kitchen manufacturing business continued to expand and prosper despite continued severe official and media pressure that would have almost certainly brought any other business to despair and bankruptcy.

Only a character of amazing resilience, strength and determination could carry a business through such storms and continue to succeed. How on earth did the man do it?

# Chapter One
## *Tough Guy*

I enter Maple Mill in Oldham. Vance Miller bounds forward with a firm handshake and careful eyes that relax when they see no threat. Muscular and fit he moves with ease and confidence, a tough guy well able to take care of himself.

He is proud of The Mill and leads me on a tour. We walk and he talks, telling the history of this 19$^{th}$ century redbrick cotton mill; four ancient floors once home to the clatter of cotton gins and clogs, now a silent store packed with the makings of modern kitchens. Vance talks in a torrent of words, hurrying through explanations and descriptions, concentrating always on two subjects – kitchens and himself.

When he talks he swears but somehow the swearing is inoffensive punctuation underlining a point or stressing a syllable – Manchester man telling a story as best he knows how. Fluent and logical in all he says, laughing at his own follies; grinding out insults and scorn on enemies and fools past and present.

"Bought the place from some daft bastard lawyer in London. He wanted more than I could afford but it was derelict – a wreck

– and the stupid sod didn't give a toss about anything north of Watford. Never came up to see the place so I offered half a million and the boneheaded idiot took it."

He'd borrowed more than needed to buy The Mill so used the extra few hundred thousand to expand his kitchen business at high speed.

This guy is a natural-born entrepreneur. At the age of eleven he started selling cheap chocolate biscuits to school friends. Using these early profits he moved into food production, buying redundant ex-battery chickens from the market, feeding them a cheap mixture of hen food and stale bread with added coal grit as a shell stiffener. His flock of fifteen old and exhausted birds rallied enough to supply sixty eggs a week for sale to his school kitchen. Along with chocolate biscuit sales he found himself making five pounds a week clear profit and decided to become a millionaire.

He left school and became a teenage antiques dealer in Manchester market. Naïve and inexperienced he happily sold stolen goods, protesting the ignorance of an 18 year old when the police came by. "I was just a young lad. I didn't know it was a crime." After fifteen months in prison he returned to the market and continued from where he left off in the stolen goods trade. "They'd asked me to stop but I didn't. Buying so cheap and selling at good prices I'd have been stupid to give up."

Caught again at the age of 22 led to his second brush with Manchester courts and he served two years of a three-year sentence. "Spending twenty-three hours a day on my bed in jail really screwed my head on tight. I lay there thinking and planning what to do when I got out and how to go straight."

He returned to selling jewellery in the markets and, aged 28, moved into gold bullion. One big deal led him to Sierra Leone where, on impulse, he bought two gold mines and a diamond mine. "A bad move 'cos that was just before the civil war and I dropped really deep in the shit."

Following two months jail in Florida, for importing unlicensed diamonds, he was arrested smuggling gold from Belgium to Britain but acquitted of any wrongdoing.

Around this time, his interest turned to kitchens whilst helping a friend away on holiday. Vance's sharp mind saw that sales of his friend's second-hand ovens and hobs would increase by advertising in more than one newspaper. Vance joined his friend's business and soon found that extra advertising and sales brought a shortage of second-hand supply, a problem Vance overcame with a trip to Milan and a deal to buy new ovens and hobs in bulk from several factories. He began importing full container loads. Business prospered.

Many of his new oven and hob customers wanted kitchens

too so Vance raised his sights and started buying up reject and second-hand kitchens for sale at knockdown prices. Expansion came fast. Within a year he built a large but ramshackle operation containing all the ingredients of both his future riches and future troubles.

The idea of buying cheap reject kitchens from big companies, tarting them up, then going into competition with your suppliers works for only a short time. So Vance broke with his business partner, took on premises and with absolutely no industrial experience started manufacturing kitchens, using ancient second-hand machinery. Two years passed before Vance managed to master both dodgy machinery and production skills.

Despite this shaky beginning, clever advertising and attractive low prices brought a flood of cash but also a flood of complaints – shoddy work, badly packed or broken deliveries, missing parts and bitter arguments with customers. "That was all years ago," says Vance. "I was selling shit stuff then but now my kitchens are great."

No matter what he says now the bad reputation lingers, spiced by a whiff of his previous criminality always used by press and television to revile Vance at every opportunity. "And the police always think I'm up to something. The bastards follow, stop or arrest me all the time and always for nothing. I'd be treated better if I killed someone or dealt in drugs instead of kitchens."

According to Vance, Maple Mill itself is part of the reason for continual media attacks that portray him as the Worst Rogue Trader in Britain – a dishonest and notorious fraud with thousands of complaints per year and dissatisfied customers clamouring at his gates every day. He is certain that the Trading Standards authorities act as the spearhead of a calculated attack.

"Why do they do this?" he asks, 'Because fookin' Oldham council want my Mill and because I saw off MFI. Those poor bastards couldn't compete with my kitchen prices and had to give up. If instead of sitting on their fat arses they'd gone to China like me and struggled round the country on those awful roads and beaten the Chinese at their own price game and bought granite quarries and forests and built factories and kept whole villages going with work like I have, perhaps they'd still be selling kitchens.

Vance is certainly able to express himself in clear and simple language but how, with legal eyes watching his every move for the past ten years has he managed – so far – to survive, stay afloat and expand? "Hard work, mate. Hard work and giving customers what they want."

## Chapter Two
## *The Mill*

Clambering between floors up a steep stone staircase I stumble on uneven steps and nearly fall. Vance laughs and says, "Think what it was like for all those poor mill girls bashing up and down here in those old clogs. I'll bet they saw a few broken bones."

"When was the place built?" I ask.

"Sometime between 1890 and 1900."

I stop and listen. My imagination conjures the clatter and giggles of girls in smocks and caps skipping between floors on stiff wooden shoes and the shivering whine of steam-operated cotton spinners turning out Victorian prosperity.

Vance's mill – two massive Victorian red brick buildings standing at right angles – dominates the centre of Oldham. I comment on the position and the fantastic view over the town and valley.

"That's my big problem," says Vance. "The council have been trying to get me out for years. They've got this great big development plan to close me down and flatten everything then change this whole area into poncy modern shops and flats. I've got a copy of their big plan. See those two other mills over there? Those businesses were doing ok until the council came along and pushed them out."

"How?"

"They found reasons, like allowing their buildings to become unsafe. They made demands that pushed the businesses into bankruptcy. Come on. Keep walking and you'll see what I've got here."

Vance hurries me into a great vaulted spinning room, now silent and stacked high with kitchen parts – doors and cupboards and drawers and shelves, all square and tidy on pallets.

I look round and say, "Christ, this is a hell of a lot of stock."

"This is only one room. I've got four floors like this holding two million doors, among all the other gear."

"Is it paid for?"

"Everything. How do you think I keep my prices so low?"

He slips a cupboard door from its pack. "Look. Real wood from my forest in Mongolia. I ship it to a village in China and they make the doors for me. I keep the whole village going. Without me they'd hardly eat. When I visit I'm treated like royalty. What a difference from here in Oldham."

He laughs and says, "Feel the wood. Beautiful eh? And look at how they put the joints together. All hand finished. Why?

Because they've no machinery to make joints. Every man in the village is a carpenter so they put the doors together by hand. And *this* gets me in trouble here at home. I was taken to court because my advertisement called it real wood – which it is. Some silly bugger thought that meant carved from one piece of wood and complained. Magistrate threw it out but said I must be careful with descriptions in future. So there's another Vance-Miller-Is-A-Crook headline in the paper."

We pass from floor to floor, through rooms piled with washing machines, driers, dishwashers and taps and piping. The whole mill – packed to the rafters with stock and equipment – is a revelation.

"All paid for," says Vance, "So don't ask again."

Vance finds it difficult not to trade. Swept up in the enthusiasm of a good deal he shipped a load of Mini Quad Bikes from China only to be charged because the Oldham authorities say the design is illegal in Britain. "So I'm soon back in court for that. You can see how the bastards try to get me at every turn."

And he couldn't resist the chance of cheap ready-made suits and shoes. "The shoes are fine and selling well but the suits are a problem. I'm a good average size so I had myself measured up and told 'em to make all the suits one size. But the stupid Chinese tailors made the jackets in inches and the trousers in centimetres so the jackets fit but the trousers are like shorts. I laugh now but I'd have killed the daft bastards if they been here in Oldham. Anyway, I told 'em to have another go at the trousers and send them separately. Fingers crossed they get it right this time."

Vance is a great storyteller, fluent and witty, his use of language colourful, descriptive and logical. Laughing always at himself and his recklessness he looks on the past as fun and the future as bright and with great pride in the mill. "This place has made me. Without it I'd still be struggling in that bloody awful old shop I started with in Manchester."

Always looking to push the business as far and fast as possible, he moved in quick succession from a terraced house in Bury to an old, almost derelict shop in Manchester then to a small mill back in Bury. "I filled the place with kitchen crap then went to work selling it."

Clever advertising brought many customers and business boomed. Starting with three workers, seventeen-year-old twin girls and a teenage boy. "We sold kitchens – or at least ninety per cent of a kitchen – to everyone from Liverpool to Leeds. But that last ten per cent of a kitchen we just couldn't get right."

Buying end-of-lines and seconds, Vance had no control over stock or quality. He groans and says, "Always running out of some part or other and not knowing when the next delivery would come I left customers all over Lancashire and Yorkshire with not quite a whole kitchen. I described us as the Kitchens From Hell but customers kept coming because of my prices and in no time I had ten people working round the clock sending out absolute rubbish. I remember one cabinet door that had a chunk missing. It was the last door of that size so I sticky-taped on a bit of wood and sent it anyway."

"Did you get complaints?"

"God, yes! We had people coming round and threatening us. One family brought a gang and lined up in the yard to fight us but my guys were bigger than their guys so they backed down. I gave them some money as compensation and they went away happy. That was when I realised I could sell kitchens but perhaps not this shit. So I decided to try better."

Vance gave up buying and trading in damaged goods. Moving to a bigger mill in Rochdale he started buying properly built kitchens from regular manufacturers.

"Did your bad reputation move with you?"

"It's never left me. With proper kit we increased sales from eight to twenty kitchens a day and rising. Then our suppliers kept letting us down so we, in turn, kept pissing off the public because we'd outgrown our supply chain. So I started to manufacture for myself."

Vance bought machinery from a bankrupt kitchen company and started producing cabinets and doors.

"What a nightmare that was for the next year or so. I knew nothing about manufacturing doors and cabinets but here I was making them. The doors used to peel; the edge-bander broke down a dozen or more times every day; the saw couldn't cut straight. No wonder the company that owned these machines went bankrupt."

"Did it worry you?"

"Of course it did. Everything I owned was in the business. I had to make it work but once again I was pissing off the public. Don't get me wrong, not every kitchen was a disaster. There were a few good ones but not many. With twenty kitchens a day going out and pre-historic machines breaking down every hour I found myself day and night in the mill trying to keep it going. Eventually I sorted it out, with the machines and factory working properly but by then my reputation was gone to hell and has never properly recovered."

But sales continued to rise and at forty kitchens a day things again began to go wrong.

"My machines couldn't make enough and my mill was a tip – far too small for the level of business I'd reached. So once again I was pissing customers off with late or cancelled deliveries and missing pieces. I knew I could sell a lot more than forty a day and needed a bigger mill. I spent a year going out every night looking at mills for sale before coming across what seemed the most humongous mill I'd ever seen – something I could only ever dream of owning."

The place – abandoned after the fabric company owning it went bankrupt – seemed perfect. Vance calculated a value of one million pounds and in a state of high excitement called his bank.

"They offered me a loan of seven hundred thousand so I'm racking my head as to where I can find the other three hundred thou'. I phoned the bankruptcy administrator in London. This guy is in his posh office in London City. He's never seen this knackered old mill in Oldham and thinks everyone north of Birmingham is a fookin' farmer. To him this mill is just a statistic on a piece of paper or a few clicks on his calculator. To me it's everything I ever dreamed of to build my business but thank God he doesn't know that. When he tells me they need six hundred thousand I can't believe my ears. I take a deep breath and tell him he's dreaming and offer five hundred thou'. He says no, but he'd take five-fifty. I say, 'You're still dreaming,' and stick at five hundred. I say 'Final offer. Take it or leave it. I'll lose no sleep while you're deciding.' Of course I didn't sleep a wink that night, dreaming about this wonderful building called Maple Mill. Next morning the phone rings and it's this idiot from London telling me he'll accept five hundred thousand."

"So in four years between 1995 and 2000 you moved from a tiny business in a shop to owning one of the biggest mills in Lancashire?"

"Amazing hey? From almost nothing to quite something in forty-eight months – I took a couple weeks before coming down to earth. Mind you, we had to work fookin' hard. We emptied our new mill of all its crap and started filling the place with kitchens. It was beautiful. We had space to move, space to manufacture and space to check kitchens before they went out. It wasn't long until we were selling more than fifty kitchens a day and things were running smoothly. I needed a proper name for the business and as the word 'Maple' scrolled across both mill towers in big white bricks I saved a fortune on sign writing by calling the company 'Maple Industries'."

At that point 'the mill' became 'The Mill' to everyone who spoke of it and it was The Mill that shot Vance's business into startling expansion and brought a whole new raft of trading and legal troubles, along with the titles 'Kitchen Gangster,' 'The Most Complained About Trader In Britain' and 'Rogue Trader'.

# Chapter Three
## *Crime and Time*

Vance lives in Cemetery Lodge, an old Victorian gatehouse. On this wet grey morning I look through rain-dribbled windows at ancient moss-covered gravestones that peek back through damp mist.

Before starting his trade in kitchens and long before buying The Mill Vance spent almost twenty years earning his living as a criminal. He's promised to tell me all about it. I wonder if he will? Last night when I started my questions on the subject his mood changed. He became grumpy and clammed up. I went to bed with a promise to try again in the morning.

He finishes breakfast, sits in a chair and stares at me.

"Well?" he says.

I decide to start hesitantly.

"A major part of your…story is your…*acknowledged* criminal past. Now…if you can tell me about that."

"Yeah."

It seems a non-aggressive "Yeah" so I continue.

"You started off in the…um…jewellery business. Did the…

what we'll call your criminality…did that start then?

"No. My first criminal charge was for handling a Belisha beacon. You know, those big yellow balls…"

"What, did you do; sell it?"

"Well, it rolled down the street and I picked it up…"

He laughs and I see him relax so interrupt and say, "Ok. But go to the true criminality, rather than the joke."

"Yeah, but it's true. That was my first criminal charge."

He laughs again so I say, "Interesting but move on to…"

"Ok. I was in the jewellery business. A young kid buying and selling mostly second-hand jewellery and dealing antiques in King Street Market, Manchester."

"What year was this?"

"Gosh, I was just short of my sixteenth birthday." He stops; frowns; calculates. "Nineteen-eighty-two. Yeah. That's right in nineteen-eighty-two I had a stall in the market and I was getting offered jewellery from burglars."

"And you knew they were burglars?

"At the time I knew it was stolen but right at the beginning I didn't know they were burglars. If you get offered something for a hundred pounds and you can sell it for two hundred pounds you take it. But when they come back a second time you start to think, 'Well, hey-up…you've come back again…' but I actually didn't think that buying stolen goods was a crime."

"You had no idea?"

"None. I thought *nicking* it was a crime. I was stupid to the extent that I'd walk through Manchester City centre with stolen candlesticks hanging out of a bag. I foolishly thought that I wasn't encouraging them. Looking back on it, if you buy stuff off a burglar you're encouraging him to go burglar again."

"When were you caught?"

"Oh, within a few months."

"What were you charged with – receiving and handling?"

"Yeah. I got eighteen months and did twelve in youth custody."

"What age were you?"

"Seventeen."

"Did going to jail shake you?"

"Yeah. It was awful. The first jail was Armley Jail and I saw things I never thought possible. At that age it all seemed so horrible."

"So this was the shock?"

"Well, I'm like, 'Fook me, I'm a kid in here and I've seen this sort of thing in films like Scum and whatnot where they show the horrors of jail and I'm *seeing* it all in real life at seventeen years of age. Right here in this jail'"

"So you did your time and what then? You went back to the

jewellery trade?"

"Yeah. I went back to the jewellery and foolishly, started buying stolen stuff again."

"It didn't occur to you that you'd be caught a second time?"

"I suppose I didn't – well obviously I didn't but I was and went back into jail for three years but I think I did two."

"Was that also a shock?"

"No. This time I was used to it but that sentence – that prison sentence – was the one when I really decided there's no future in crime."

"You decided not to be a criminal?"

"Yes"

"And you've not been a criminal since."

"No. Not ever, *ever* since have I committed a dishonest crime. I knew I wanted out. Sitting on a prison bed for twenty-three hours a day I decided what I wanted from life was a mobile 'phone, a Porsche and to spend the day driving round inspecting my shops and things like that and I thought to myself, 'How do I get started?'"

So out of prison and completely broke, Vance puts earlier brief experience in selling double-glazing to work.

"Although only a kid I'd become the company's top window salesman so I tried to implement the double-glazing technique in jewellery. I became a man on the road, a man on a bike, going round the streets selling. I had a grand's worth of jewellery that manufacturers in Birmingham gave me on credit and came back to Manchester and went round selling to small jewellers. After a while the manufacturers began to trust me…"

"Did they know of your criminal past?"

"Oh yeah. I told 'em. It seemed the best way for them to find out and after a while I was carrying up to a hundred grand's worth of jewellery on credit. Off I'd go and sell it then go and pay the guys in Birmingham, and then I'd have a hundred-and-twenty grand's worth to sell and it just built up. At last I was making and saving good money in business built on trust. I was supplying wholesale jewellery around Lancashire and Yorkshire. A lot fookin' different from being a criminal."

"But you were involved twice more in criminal activity, smuggling diamonds and gold."

"Oh yes. So I was. The diamonds were the biggest problem and gave me the biggest fright.""

## Chapter Four
# *The American Diamond Caper*

Vance rubs a hand over his eyes and says, "Those diamonds. Oh those fookin' diamonds. It happened in America. I had these diamonds from South Africa."

"Here in England?"

"Yeah. And for some strange reason thought that, perhaps, I could sell them in America"

"Were the diamonds legal?"

"No."

"How did they arrive here?"

"They were brought by Africans."

"South Africans?"

"Yeah. Black South Africans. They steal them there and smuggle them here. I pay cash and they're quite happy. They get money and I get cheap diamonds. And at this stage I convince myself I'm not hurting anybody. Who on earth is suffering from my crime? Nobody. And I was never caught here in Britain."

So Vance assures himself that this is clean crime. He finds sales for the diamonds in Britain but decides to try smuggling into

America for, perhaps, a better price.

"I went with my mate and when we got to American Customs I see a young girl on the counter and show her some rings I took as samples to try and get orders. She says, 'Where are you staying?' so off the top of my head I tells her the Holiday Inn. She says 'The Holiday Inn on Orlando Drive?' I've never heard of the place but to go along with her, I says, 'Yes, that's the one,' and she says 'Ok. I'll meet you there at eight o'clock this evening and we'll go through what you've got."

"She let you a free pass through Customs with nothing but a promise to meet later?"

"Yeah. And I thinks, '*What*? A Customs lady wants to meet me later at the hotel?' but I says, 'Ok then,' and make an arrangement to meet her at eight-thirty and goes and gets in the car and says to my mate, 'Shit, man, we'd better go and book in to the Holiday Inn at Orlando Drive and meet her there."

"Did she turn up?"

"Yeah. She was lovely. She charged us a hundred-and-eighty dollars import duty because the rings were just samples and we promised to take them out again when we went home. Then she offered to help and take us round to some antiques fairs and markets and what-not and next morning she met us – it was a weekend – and took us around some places. She was a lovely lady.

She even came swimming with me. I think she must have fancied me or something."

"I've never heard of anything like this."

"Me neither."

"Did she ask for anything? Any bribe or, perhaps, a diamond or two."

"No. Nothing. She just wanted to help us and everything was great. After a while she left and my mate and me started going to places on our own."

Vance called on several shops and started selling the illegal diamonds. After the third or fourth call, when packing his bag he realised a pouch of loose stones had been left, by accident, in the previous shop.

"How many did you leave?"

"About a hundred grand's worth, so I rang and asked for my diamonds back. 'What diamonds?' the guy says, "I ain't got your diamonds.' So I say, 'Hey-up, one of those hey?' and wondered, 'What the hell am I going to do? I can either report it to the police or fly in some heavies in from England and take my diamonds back off him.'"

"Which did you do?"

"Both. Like an idiot I did both. I reported it to the police and I arranged for some heavies to come out. The heavies arrived on the Friday but the day before that I was sitting on this jet ski in some guy's garden when seventy or eighty armed police in *loads* of cars came in shouting, 'Are you Vance Miller,' and my American friend said, 'You'd better tell them who you are Vance,' so I did and they arrested me."

"What happened then?"

"Well, the police said, 'These diamonds you've been selling – you never declared them,' and I thought, 'Yeah, and what a fookin' prick I am,' so they locked me up in Seminole County jail for three months."

"Three months?"

"Yeah."

"Not good?"

"It was shit. I'd already experienced British jails at this stage so I knew what jail was all about. I was in a Federal prison where you have to wear orange suits and when you're moved they shackle your hands and feet with chains so when you go to court for a simple enquiry you can hardly walk. It's ridiculous. It's just like slavery."

"What about the actual prison?"

Vance screws his face up and thinks. "Well…it was like a circle and each block was cut into half a circle and all round your half-circle were two levels with all these cages with bars that close

– boom – at night and they open in the morning. So you were restricted to this place and the only exercise you had was walking round the half-circle or up and down the stairs, doing whatever exercise you could. And for about an hour a day you were allowed out into the exercise yard. It was red hot at the time and they had pull-up bars and dip bars and just like a conventional gym on the exercise yard, so you managed to get some exercise there. And the food was awful – every morning you got this most disgusting peanut butter in the world."

"Peanut butter with what?"

"Do you know, I can't remember…"

"With bread?"

Vance twists his face again and rubs his chin, "Do you know I can't remember. This fookin' awful peanut butter is just stuck in my mind. I can't think of anything else…"

"And what about other prisoners? We hear terrible tales of American prisons. How did you get on with the people in there?"

"I got on great. But I remember this black guy who was in my cell at first. For some reason he took a shine to my trainers. He wanted to be cock of the cell and I put up with it for the first couple of days but in the end – I don't know what he wanted – I think he had an idea of putting on my trainers and waltzing round the cell to show off. Anyway we had this great argument."

"Did you smack him one?"

"No. Nothing like that; we just had this great argument and that stopped it. He was fine after that."

"And what about the other prisoners? What did they think about having an Englishman in the prison?"

"Well, I was different, wasn't I. But it was no problem and I just kept quiet and got on with being there. One guy I met – Mike, a cocaine dealer –became my friend and when after three months I got bail and had to stay in America he gave me the keys to his house – a beautiful, beautiful house. I lived in his house for a couple of months then did a deal with the prosecution, 'You keep the diamonds and I'll sod off home,'"

"How did you get to know Mike?"

"Well I was locked up in that half-circle and when it's like that you get to meet those who're the same sort of level as you and he became my pal. So when I got bail and told him they might make me stay in America he said, 'Use my house. There's a girl called Madonna with the keys. See her and get the keys and use the house as if it's your own.' So I got bail, went and got the keys and opened up the house and – fook me – what a place, with this wonderful fountain going in the foyer as you walked in and a proper bachelors penthouse suite; black leather sofas, black velvet all over the walls, fantastic music systems, water beds, hundreds of CDs on shelves all over the walls; a communal gym downstairs, swimming pools and all that. I thought, bloody hell, I've landed on my feet here, haven't I?

"How long did you stay?"

"About two months. He never asked me for a penny in rent and I brought my Mum and my cousin over for a holiday. They loved it."

"And while you were in the house did you come across any of his drug-dealing friends?"

"No."

"Nobody came to see you?"

"No."

"So there were no hints that anyone could say you were involved in his drug deals?"

"No."

"Did you ever meet Mike again?"

"No, but I read an article a few years ago about a guy called Mike, with exactly the same second name. He'd been shot dead by a drug dealer and I hoped it wasn't my mate."

"But you never saw or heard from him again?"

"No."

"So after a couple of months living in Mike's house on bail, you were taken back to court as a felon to make the deal to let you leave if you surrendered the diamonds?"

"No. We never got to court."

"Not at all?"

"No. We were in an office."

"So how did you negotiate the deal?"

Vance giggles…"I said you keep the diamonds and I'll just go…"

"Yes, but the question is; were you negotiating with police agents or Customs agents?"

"Customs. Two or three of 'em; the same ones that originally arrested me."

"Including the woman who allowed you in and introduced you to diamond dealers?"

"No. She wasn't there."

My question brought the whole memory of his arrival in America back to Vance's mind. In some agitation he jumps up and cries, "Yeah, that Customs lady who took me to antique fairs and even went swimming with me? What was *that* all about? Can you imagine appearing at Customs and saying I have things to declare and her saying don't pay me the duty now; I'll meet you later. I'll come to your hotel. Then she takes me swimming and to *antique fairs?* Can you imagine it – just letting me walk out of the airport and coming to my hotel later?"

"Yes, but do you think she suspected you then?"

"Nope."

"Were the diamonds you agreed to leave behind with these Customs people the ones you lost or other diamonds?"

"The ones that were nicked I never saw again but I had loads of other diamonds when Customs arrested me. Those were the ones they held on to."

"So they just agreed to let you go; gave you your passport back and…"

"Yeah. Off you go. And don't come back."

"Do you have any suspicion that the three Customs officers and the very helpful woman you met first may have kept the diamonds for themselves? I mean stole them from you?

Opening his mouth to reply Vance shaped the word 'No' then stopped, frowning before saying very slowly, "I've never thought about that…"

"What do you think now? Because you say you never came before a judge – the deal to let you go was done in an office with only those Customs officers present."

"You're right. I came before a judge only at the beginning for remand purposes and never went to court again. The actual deal to let me go was done out of court and they said, 'Go', so I buggered off. At the time I thought they just wanted to wash their hands of me because I wasn't American so the deal they made was, 'We'll keep the diamonds and you fook off."

"So you never thought it may be a scam so they could keep and sell the diamonds?"

After another pause, Vance says, "I never thought about it before but now you've asked me…" He shakes his head, perhaps in admiration at so neat a trick.

I ask, "Well, what do you think now?"

Still caught up in the trick they may have pulled he almost chuckles and says, "Well somebody's got 'em haven't they? I haven't got 'em. Yeah. Now I think about it I wonder what ever happened to them diamonds."

"Well it seems to me they ran a scam on you."

Vance shrugs with a laugh and says, "Well, it's the deal they came up with isn't it? You leave the diamonds and fook off. So I did."

"I still think that perhaps your young Customs lady didn't fancy you at all. Perhaps she saw you as a smuggler and set a trap?"

"Now I think of it you could be right."

"But you didn't learn a lesson from all this. You went home to England and started to smuggle gold."

"Yeah. How stupid can you be?"

# Chapter Five
## *The Belgian Gold Caper*

Vance leans back and laughs. "The gold caper was really odd and nearly put me back in jail again. I came real close to going back inside."

Finding they could trust Vance, the Birmingham suppliers he refers to as 'The Jews' asked him to sell gold alongside the jewellery.

"The Jews cottoned on to the fact that I had balls. They'd say, 'My kids are schmuks. Why can't they be like you?' and started to use me. They'd trust me with half a million worth of gold and give me three or four days to go and sell it round dealers and wholesalers in Yorkshire and Lancashire."

Vance soon realised he was part of a sophisticated tax fraud. "I think this was around nineteen-ninety and at that time gold was free of VAT in Belgium, so cheaper than in England.

The way Vance describes it, "The Jews" bought gold in Belgium at "two per cent over market price," and hired carriers who smuggled it to Britain. Vance then took the gold and sold at between three and six per cent profit, plus VAT to shady dealers and wholesalers willing to pay slightly above market price.

"As soon as the gold arrived I'd pick it up and over three or four days get it to people who used a newly opened company to sell the gold plus VAT. They then claimed the VAT back before closing that company owing millions of pounds tax and opening another one. That way everyone made money out of the VAT man."

"Did you go to Belgium to collect the gold?"

"No I met it when it got into England, so I wasn't actually smuggling."

The scam seemed simple and worked well but soon came to an end.

I ask, "How long were you doing this?"

"About a year. Then they got onto us when the carrier – the guy that did the smuggling - got nicked at Dover, carrying the gold. Customs used him to work on finding the wider conspiracy and so one Jew got nicked and so did I. The three of us were charged."

"And what about the people to whom you sold – the other end of the scam? Did they get nicked?"

"No. Mind you, they didn't get me at first. I ran off to Scotland but handed myself in after a week."

"So you were charged in court for that but somehow got off."

"Yeah."

"How?"

"The prosecution relied on mobile telephone evidence. When the smuggler arrived in the country he'd 'phone me and I'd 'phone various bullion dealers --."

"Your 'phone was tapped?"

"No.", says Vance. "They had computer charts and logs showing the smuggler calling me and me calling bullion dealers and they followed that path. But then Alan Neal, lawyer for the carrier caught at Dover, saw a hole in the prosecution case and argued that for computer evidence to be relied on in court it must show that the telephone companies' computers were working properly. The judge agreed and brought the operators from my airtime companies to give evidence."

This is where the prosecution case began to fall apart. Computer operators from the airtime companies supplying Vance's mobile telephones, Unique Air and Martin Dawes Air, came to court and confirmed their equipment was operating correctly at the time the prosecution log showed.

But Alan Neal argued the evidence was hearsay because their systems, being at the end of an airtime supply chain, worked on second-hand information. These two suppliers bought airtime from a couple of large national companies, Vodaphone and Cell

Net, and sold it on to Vance Miller as end user. So the evidence put forward by Unique Air and Martin Dawes Air was indirect.

Alan Neal later told me, "As Vance said, the prosecution relied heavily upon traffic between mobile telephones of the three accused. They produced vast schedules showing that at the relevant times all three accused had regularly contacted one another, a fact which was incapable, in all the circumstances, of innocent explanation.

"However, at that time, under a provision of the Police and Criminal Evidence Act 1984, the law required that the side calling evidence from computer sources needed to show the relevant computer from which the data had been *gathered* was functioning properly. When I looked into this aspect of the Crown's case I saw the evidence they relied on came from service providers not network providers. Network providers create and operate the networks that enable telephone calls to be made whereas service providers merely *purchase* airtime from network providers, which they then resell. Naturally, the service providers rely upon data from the original network provider to determine the telephone numbers of callers and recipients and the duration of calls. Equally naturally, all such data, so far as the *service* providers were concerned, is hearsay.

"The only people able to guarantee proper functioning of the relevant computers were those in the *network* providers. From them no evidence was forthcoming.

"On behalf of my client I advanced the argument that all telephone evidence produced by the prosecution was inadmissible hearsay and failed to identify the relevant computer or computers so therefore incapable of showing that properly functioning equipment was being used as the law at that time required.

"The judge adjourned the case to enable prosecution to bring witnesses from the original network providers. This prosecution failed to do, so the judge reluctantly conceded my argument as correct and excluded all telephone evidence. This left the prosecution with a gaping hole in its conspiracy charge case. Eventually the Crown gave up and offered no further evidence. The judge immediately directed a verdict of not guilty be entered against all three accused on the conspiracy count. But unfortunately, as my client had been caught in the act of smuggling, he had to plead guilty to that aspect.

"Vance and the other defendant, both somewhat bemused, were promptly released. Each had separate representation that had failed to notice the lacuna I spotted. I heard later that word of our case went round the court like wildfire and that within hours two major drugs cases, reliant upon similar evidence ended in an identical manner. Indeed, for about two years it remained possible to use the same strategy until Section 69 of the act was eventually repealed."

"So," says Vance, "The judge kicked the case out."

"But although the case was thrown out of court on that very clever approach, you were in fact guilty."

"Yeah."

"And that was the last time you did any criminality?"

"Yeah. I never, ever, *ever*, bought a stolen item since. If someone comes to me now with something I won't have anything to do with it. I'm in a wonderful position now where I can afford not to involve myself in criminality, but…em… I don't want to encourage them criminals now. I don't want someone's house to be burgled."

"So this is truly the time you gave up crime and decided to stick to proper and honest business."

"Yes."

"Just as well. You seem to have been a pretty inefficient criminal, always being caught. But you seem to have turned into a brilliant businessman."

"Yeah. Funny isn't it."

"And do you know, during the recording of these criminal stories, you've hardly sworn at all."

"Fook me, haven't I?"

# Chapter Six
## *African Adventure*

Sitting with Vance after a relaxed dinner in Cemetery Lodge, I ask, "What made you go to Africa? Sierra Leone, wasn't it?"

In mellow mood after a few drinks he rubs his face and stares through the window at damp gravestones glistening in yellow lamplight.

"Oh, God," he says. "What an idiot. I nearly ended up in one of them graves."

"But you're a kitchen man. What on earth were you doing gallivanting round Africa? Looking to buy wood or something for kitchens?"

"No. Gold. I met this guy called Alan who said if I give him fifty grand he'd send it to Sierra Leone where he could buy gold for thirty to forty percent less than market value. So I explained to him, 'Look Alan, you're much more of a shrewd man than me but there's no way you can buy gold that cheap.' So he tried to convince me it was a government scam and that sort of thing and I said, 'I don't give a damn who's scam it is, gold has an international value and nobody sells gold at less than market value.' So Alan goes red and starts shouting 'No-no-no,' at me.'"

I watch Vance reliving the argument with raised voice and stabbing finger to interrupt Alan, "I'll tell you what – there's no way on this earth I'm parting with fifty grand to *you* but book me two tickets and I'll get myself a bodyguard and we'll go out to Africa and see how we go from there."

"It sounds similar to those Nigerian con jobs," I say. "Why did you actually have to go?"

Vance shouts, "To shut him up. The stupid bastard kept going on at me."

I snap back, "Yes but my question is different. Why did you have to go since most of these West African scams are based on money going into banks in Europe?"

"Because I knew for a fact that if I put my money into this I'd never ever see it again and I was saying, 'Please, Alan, get your head round it that this gold price is not true,' but he was convinced that this was a proper deal so I said, 'Book the two tickets and I'll go out there and prove to you it's just a load of bullshit.'"

This crazy conversation with Alan took place in the mid-nineties with Vance just out of jail and already started in kitchens but it seems he could not resist this new, quite stupid challenge.

So Alan bought two tickets and Vance prepared to go. "I got myself a bodyguard, Dave, my best mate at the time who I trained with in the gym. He was a big heavy bastard, about two-hundred-and-seventy pounds of sheer muscle. And I looked the part as well, 'cos I'd just got out of jail where I spent a lot of time in the prison gym. So I borrowed a couple of bulletproof vests and got my gold testing equipment..."

I interrupted to ask, "Had the Sierra Leone civil war already started?"

"No."

"So why the bulletproof vests?"

"Because I knew I was entering in to a dangerous place and these guys may try to have me over."

So Vance flew to Africa with his bulletproof vests, his bodyguard and gold testing equipment, ready for anything. Or so he thought. At first all went as he expected when three smartly dressed men met him at Freetown Airport.

"I didn't trust the bastards the minute I saw them. They pretended we were important visitors and all that crap. They whisked us straight through Customs and Immigration without stopping – real red carpet treatment – and drove us to the centre of Freetown and said, 'Right, we're putting you in the city's main hotel.' I said, 'No, no, we'll get our own hotel,' and they said,

'No you must go in this hotel,' so we stood there arguing with me saying, 'We'll find our own hotel where you don't know where we are,' so after a lot of blagging they allowed us to find our own hotel."

Vance and bodyguard found a hotel at the beach, a place with separate chalets scattered among palm trees. "So," says Vance, "I had one of these with a little fan and a bathroom in it and then came the first meeting with these guys. They were sort of Syrian."

"Syrian? Do you mean Lebanese?"

"Yeah. Lebanese. I saw a lot of them in Sierra Leone."

"Were any Africans involved?"

"In the room or in the scam?"

"In the scam."

"Yeah. These Lebanese were working together with Africans. And they had one bodyguard in the room when we met."

The meeting turned into a prickly affair. Vance took a few photographs of these Lebanese and their bruiser – an enormous African who sat glowering in a corner. No one in the picture looks happy.

"So anyway," says Vance. "We're in this hotel room and they say, 'Give us fifty grand and we'll go and get the gold.' I says, 'No it don't work like that. I'm going to give you five hundred quid. When you come back with five hundred quids worth of gold I'll export it immediately. Then tomorrow I'll give you money for two grand-worth of gold and export that, then I'll buy five grand-worth and export that…"

"You were, at this point, carrying cash?"

"Not on me. No. They knew I had money but not cash on me. I'd wired it to a Sierra Leone bank and later lost half but that's another story.

So Vance argued for a while with the Lebanese, explaining that each individual daily purchase would increase, from five to ten thousand then twenty thousand until the fifty thousand deal concluded over a week to ten days.

"Did the Lebanese like this idea?"

"No, not at all. They wanted the fifty grand right now. They said they wanted a long-term relationship built on trust and all that bullshit. I said, 'What's the difference? In a week you'll have all the money and I'll have the gold and then we'll be able to trust each other.' But no, they weren't having it so I got onto the 'phone to Alan and said 'I'm stuck in this hotel room with these Lebanese scam merchants.'"

He laughs, shakes his head and says, "I'll always remember that hotel room with them blokes there."

"And they were listening to the telephone call?"

"Yeah. They were all listening and I shouted to Alan, 'They're all fookin' scam merchants, that's all they are – end of story – I'll have nothing more to do with it,' so the meeting ended and they walked out."

Vance returned to his beach hotel and over the next few days made friends with the young fishermen working in the area. He checked around and spent a couple of weeks visiting villages and talking to local elders and meeting Africans from the gold diggings. Once he had a feel for how it worked he bought a gold exporting licence from the Sierra Leone government and opened three shops with big signs advertising The London Gold Buying Centre and started taking in gold from local African diggers.

"Then I went back round the villages and bought gold mining rights for three areas from the village elders. So I had three shops, three gold mines and an export licence and spent my time rushing around the shops and the gold mines, often getting down into the mine and digging with my Africans."

"You actually went down into the mine and dug with your African workers?"

"Of course I did. Yeah. It wasn't a deep tunnel mine, more of a scoop in the ground – a sort of small quarry. I'd get down and dig every day for about an hour. It made them work better. I got involved in the heat of the day, digging and picking out bits of gold alongside them to keep them going." Vance chuckles and shrugs, "I wish I was still energetic enough to do all that again."

What with all the rushing around and finding himself unable to eat the local food, Vance began to lose weight fast. "I was *really* losing weight and later I lost Dave, my bodyguard, because I spent the two weeks he was there minding him, he didn't look after me one bit."

"Why? Because he became ill?"

"Yeah. He kept showing off to prostitutes and then caught malaria. He was a big bruiser but he was naïve and I sent him home. That was when I started buying mines so was doing it all by myself, not eating properly and losing weight."

Vance bought a jeep and became mobile. Finding he needed better equipment he sent to England for a set of electronic scales and in the same shipment ordered a load of protein powder to help with his weight problem.

"Meantime I'd got to know the captain of the local military police, Ronnie, an African – a real good and intelligent guy – so I was always knocking about the military police headquarters and their prefabs with my bruiser Dave and they thought we were American. They kept saying, 'The Americans are here.' But I told 'em, 'No. We're British. I'm a captain in the SAS here to help the Government. We're here to build a gym and all that shit and they believed us.'"

"So what happened to the Lebanese and the original gold deal? Did they just disappear?"

"Yeah. They just disappeared but one of their bruisers – a guy that always carried an Uzi machine gun – found out where we were staying and he used to come and poke his nose in, still trying to do the deal. He used to come with a kilo of gold – the real stuff – and want to deal but I could just tell he was a murderer, a proper scam merchant, so I wouldn't have anything to do with him. He hung around for a while then stopped coming."

"So you never saw the Lebanese again?"

"No. But what happened when the protein powder and the scales arrived at the airport I went to collect it with Ronnie the military police captain and we both got arrested."

"Arrested? Why?"

"For importing cocaine."

"But you weren't importing cocaine."

"No. And they didn't care that half of it tasted of strawberry and the other half tasted of vanilla. As far as they're concerned I'm there with this white powder and these scales so I'm a drug dealer. So both me and the captain get locked up."

"Was this Customs or Police?

"Customs. They kept us in cells for about three days then shipped us off to Freetown jail where we stayed for two days then a military coup kicks off and we all broke out. Someone opened the gate and in no time everyone is running out."

Vance starts laughing and says, "Whey-hey, we're all out, so I run off back to the hotel and I'd just got into my room when all hell breaks loose."

At this point Vance – caught up in the excitement of his story – jumps to his feet and starts rushing round the Cemetery Lodge room, acting out what happened next. I jump up and follow, waving my digital recorder as close as possible to his face as – in Sierra Leone – he grabs a camera, runs out to hide in a clump of bushes.

"Hey… I've got to get some photos of this."

He crouches in the bush to watch soldiers and militia bursting into the hotel, waving guns and machetes and rushing out with arms full of bottles, food, television sets and anything else they can lift and carry.

"So I creeps to the edge of some bushes, sticks my camera out and….Oooh! The flash went off. Wham! Oh, my God! What do I do? I had to think fast so I turned and ran for three or four seconds; hid the camera behind a tree and ran back to where I'd taken the picture from. The soldiers came rushing round shouting 'Flashy, flashy, you flashy; flashy,' and I'm standing there shouting back, 'Me no flashy, flashy, me no flashy, flashy,'

With the soldiers waving guns and closing in Vance knew he had to do something drastic, "So I waved my arms and shouted at the buggers, 'You get aggressive with me I'll get aggressive with you. You want American and British intervention you'll fookin' get it, blah, blah, blah,' so I fronted it. I stood there and fronted it really, really well and they fell for it and went away."

"So you threatened them with British and American intervention and they believed it?"

"Yeah. I couldn't do fook-all about it but they fell for it. They thought I was a soldier because I was built like one. Then all the hotel staff and guests still there came out, all relieved and excited and slapping me on the back. 'You're a hero. You're a crazy man but you're a hero.' They saw me as a security guy, a guy that can save them."

In the way of Africa, the news flew round the village that a big man – a man that can save them – lived in the hotel. "All the villagers had been out looting and every hut in the village was full of fridges and tellys and stuff they'd nicked from the white peoples' houses. Then the rebels came and started looting the looters, grabbing all the tellys and whatnot. So the villagers came running to me shouting 'Captain Miller, we're being looted, come and help."

Vance stands to attention in the middle of the Cemetery Lodge room and toots a military charge on his imaginary trumpet. "So idiot here goes running into the village, doesn't he? And that's where I come across a great big African calling himself Rambo."

He relaxes for a moment, seeing the picture in his head. "They're all there, nicking and whatnot so I stands and starts my cocky stupid speech again, blah, blah, blah and the next thing I know I'm wrestling with this huge Rambo over an AK 47 he's holding but I grabbed onto. He pulls it one-way and I pull it another with me thinking what the fook do I do now? How do I get out of this one? The only plan I could come up with was run – just *run*. So I ran. I let go of the gun and legged it as fast as I could."

Vance rushes across the room, dodging furniture, with me following; waving my recorder under his nose.

"It was dark and I ran and couldn't see anything and banged straight into a tree nose first but didn't feel a thing. I bounced off and carried on running and this guy's shooting at me and he managed to shoot me in the back of my arm."

Vance stops acting and rolls his sleeve up to show me the scar. "See. Here in the back of my arm."

I reach over and run fingers across the rough skin circle. Definitely a bullet wound. I've seen plenty of them.

The story starts again and Vance jumps back into action.

"At the time it felt just like a wasp sting. Nothing more than a wasp sting and I'm running and through my head is going, 'Africans can't swim. Africans can't swim, ' and all the time I'm running through the trees thinking, 'Get to the sea, get to the sea,' so I race down the beach and into the water and swim like fook. It's dark and after a while everything goes quiet so I go back to the hotel and realise I've got a hole, a great big hole in my arm – a really deep hole in the muscle – so I put a plaster on it. A few days later I took the plaster off and there was half a bullet showing out of the wound; my body must have kicked it out and I thought, 'Fook me, I was shot.'"

"You didn't realise at the time?"

"No. With so much happening I thought I'd done it when I ran into the tree. I kept the bullet. I brought it back in a packet with the little bit of gold I managed to mine in Sierra Leone but where the hell the packet is now I don't know. It'll be somewhere in the house."

"So was being shot the end of this goldmine episode? Did you get out of Sierra Leone straight away?"

"No. Not after all I'd done, what with nearly getting ripped off and getting shot and all. There was a battleship out at sea, an American or British or one of those lot, and a helicopter coming backward and forward evacuating all the whites and I thought to hell with this, I'm not getting evacuated. I've never seen anything like this in my life. I'm staying. Maybe I'm a bit crazy but I ain't leaving here."

So against all commonsense, Vance decided to stay. He reasoned that since the rebels held all of Freetown, the best place to be is out in the countryside.

"I had fifteen thousand pounds in a Freetown bank that the bastard rebels burnt down. And it's not like here when you can go no; no; no, and go to, like to another Barclays in another town and say, 'Excuse me, I deposited fifteen grand in Freetown and its gone', 'cos they'd say, 'That was the only bank we had, Mate. Your money's gone with it.' Great! So I left Freetown and set up in Bumbula, near one of my goldmines. I continued mining but then petrol became scarce. You need petrol to run the pumps to get all the water out and the price of petrol started doubling every day and the military just took control of all the petrol stations and nobody but military could get any. So I had to go personally down to the petrol stations and do a deal with them to fill my drums up. Then that all dried up because no one would send petrol into Sierra Leone 'cos they wouldn't get paid for it so the country ran out of petrol. So I'm sitting at my goldmine all the time watching the work and hoping I'd get more petrol but I stuck around for a bit and noticed the butterflies."

"Butterflies?"

"Yeah. Butterflies."

It may have been that the pressure of being shot, running out of petrol, running out of money, being far from home or simply being alone in Africa began to affect Vance's mind.

"What butterflies?"

"Oh in Sierra Leone you see the most beautiful butterflies in the world. Beautiful…"

Vance's looks out the window of Cemetery Lodge and sighs, probably seeing clouds of brilliant coloured African butterflies instead of gravestones.

Whatever Vance's state of mind, the butterflies took him out of Africa to eventual safety although not without further adventure and loss.

After a few moments living again among those butterflies, Vance returns to Cemetery Lodge and says, "Watching these butterflies, I got this daft idea that I could catch them – or get people catching them for me - and put them in beautiful frames and sell them. But I needed some butterfly catching equipment so I'd have to go back to England. I could leave through Freetown where all the rebels were still kicking off – but that would be hard – or I could go through Conakry in Guinea, the next country."

Vance planned to be out of Sierra Leone for only a week then back to start his butterfly business. He decided to leave through Conakry.

"I went by taxi and got dropped off at the end of Sierra Leone and there was a mile gap between the two countries' borders so I marched with my bags across to the Guinea side. In my bags I had about two thousand pounds in Sierra Leone money. Well that filled half of my big bag 'cos it was such a lot of notes."

Vance reaches the Guinea border post and runs into the West African "dash" system – the handing over of cash to complete any official action – or, indeed, any action at all.

He says, "I gets to the Guinea border post and there's this Customs guy eating rice with his fingers." Again reliving the moment, Vance squeaks, "You have no visa," in a high-pitched French African accent.

"Come off it. There's a war going on in Sierra Leone. I'm a European trying to get out through to Conakry.

"You need visa, you need visa," squeaks the African.

Of course, in searching Vance's bag the Customs man sees the money. Vance becomes angry, "Fook off. I know you want my money. You'll not get any. I'll leave through Freetown."

In high rage Vance hunches his shoulders and marches back towards Sierra Leone. "But I knew I'd have to turn round and eat humble pie with this guy after I'd thrown my dummy out of the pram and told him to go fook yourself, etc. So I sat on a rock and thought for ten minutes then goes back and throws six thousand, or whatever he wanted, on his table and he gives me a visa."

Snatching the money into his pocket the African squeaks, "And now you need police escort."

"Oh fook off. You're just after more money, I don't need no police escort."

"Yes. You need police escort to pass through Guinea. A foreigner not allowed through Guinea without police escort."

So Vance throws more money on the table and says, "Just get me out of this shit hole."

The money disappears in a flash and the Customs man squeaks, "And now you need taxi."

"I don't need taxi. I'll catch a bus."

"No-no-no you need driver."

"So I pay for a taxi and at this stage he's taken half of what I'd got in my bag and I'm ready to go and you know what he says? 'We no take Sierra Leone money here. There is war in Sierra Leone.'"

Chasing Vance round the room with my recorder, trying to catch his story and follow the act as he stalks away, marches back, crouches, bangs the table, leans across to confront his squeaky-voiced African, I can see that, for those few minutes, he is far from Lancashire, far from Cemetery Lodge. He is back in Africa, facing another danger, another problem, and another serious threat. Vance waves a fist and shouts, "Don't tell me. I know the story. You've got a clever pal who'll exchange me at two-to-one."

The African nodded 'Yeah, I have friend who can help."

Vance's shoulders drop and he deflates, and returns to be with me in Cemetery Lodge. Flopping back into his chair he says, "So they took everything off me except for a wad that big," with wide thumb and finger he indicates a pack of banknotes, "So off I finally go to Conakry."

He falls silent for a moment and sighs, "Yeah. They almost got the lot."

I ask, "Was that the end of it?"

"Not likely. Although I'd paid for petrol the taxi ran out, didn't it? So we had to walk for a few miles to buy a few bottles they sell by the roadside. Finally we got to Conakry and the airport and I'm in there, covered with sweat 'cos I've just about made the 'plane, when Customs call me into this room, don't they, and before they can speak I say, 'All right. If you're after my money, you've already had it, you've got the lot, I've got *nowt*.'"

He collapses into laughter and shakes his head. "So they let me through and I sat on the plane and thought, well, after almost four months in Sierra Leone I'm London bound at last."

"And you never went back?"

"Came home and all ready to go back I went down to Kent to the only place in England that sells butterfly catching equipment. I took Joanna and she was pregnant and we thought, what a wonderful name, Kent, let's call our kid Kent so my son is sort of named after the Sierra Leone escapade isn't he?

"But did you go back?"

Vance breaks into a rueful giggle. "Well we bought a whole lot of butterfly catching equipment and it's still here in the store room."

"So you never went back."

He shrugs. "Never went back. I sobered up and it was like, 'Ooh, you dickhead. What was *that* all about?"

"Yes. You could have been killed."

"Yeah. I had a great time though. It was three and a half months or so and there's lots more stories and I've only told you some of 'em."

"You were already in the kitchens business when you went to Sierra Leone so did you think of looking for business there?"

"Yeah. I took pictures of cabinet doors with me but nothing came of it."

"Who was running the business in England while you were in Africa?"

"During my time away, it all went to pot, really."

"Was it a big business at that time?"

"Not on the scale it is now."

"But was it the sort of business you would have been making good money on?"

"Yes. But when I got home it was on its knees."

"So what did you do about that?"

"I just worked like stink and got it back up again."

"So what you learned from all this escapade – apart from how to run and duck – was…don't go on a wild goose chase and leave a perfectly good and thriving business for too long."

"No. That's what I should have learnt but I didn't."

"So what else did you do that you shouldn't?"

"Well, I fooked off to China on a wild goose chase, didn't I? And it came up trumps."

# Chapter Seven
## *Discovering China*

Perhaps the danger and drama of Sierra Leone gave Vance a taste for foreign adventure because after a short time in the relative peace and quiet of Oldham he set off again, this time to China. Why?

"Because a mate of mine said he was going to a Beijing trade show so I thought, good idea, I'll go too."

"Just like that? On impulse?"

"Yeah. More or less but I'd heard that China is a good place for wood so I took chipboard door samples and a kitchen cabinet to get them copied into real wood. It was just before I bought Maple Mill and I knew I'd need to develop a different sort of business and realised it doesn't cost much more to improve quality."

Vance landed in South China and after a few days wandering round the trade show decided it a was waste of time. "The show was too easy for me – too formal. I thought there must be more to things than this and I wanted to go deeper into how the market is supplied. I wanted to know where these Chinese guys selling at the trade show were getting their products from."

"So you wanted to study the market aggressively – further down the supply chain – beyond the salesmen sitting on trade stands waiting for visitors."

"Yeah. I wanted more detail so I went north. I wanted to get to the forests where the wood comes from so I left my mate and flew to a town called Harbin in the north, at the top end of China. It was a week or two before Christmas and really, really cold. I got out of the plane and spent a few days just walking round in freezing snow and wind, trying to meet people who dealt in wood. It was difficult at first 'cos I didn't know nobody"

"Did you find the local people looked at you a bit strangely because you were pottering round on your own?

"Hugely. Massively, massively; and that was in Harbin a big city. Once I moved out further north they looked at me like I was like an alien who'd just landed. It was strange for me too. Odd things happened. For instance, when I arrived in Harbin the stupid taxi driver from the airport set fire to my suitcase."

"How?"

"Well he took me to a hotel and when we arrived the lock on his boot was frozen and he couldn't get it open. So he got out this gas burner and turns it on the lock and sets fire to his boot and to my luggage. The whole lid of my suitcase was all burnt along with the top layer of my clothes. That was my introduction to the place. And he put me in this hotel – I reckon he was on commission – so I parked my arse there for a few days and just went out round Harbin visiting people connected to the wood industry."

"How did you manage with the language?"

"I got by for the first few days with help from an American Chinese who lived in Harbin. Then while going round the businesses, shops and wood markets in Harbin I met Mr Lee, a wood dealer. He spoke enough English to get by and he said he knew a few factories up in the forests that could do the kind of thing I wanted. So I got on trains with him and spent a couple of weeks further north going to different forests and factories that made products out of wood. It was quite difficult. We'd spend a whole day – sometimes a day and a half – on a train then eventually get off somewhere in the middle of nowhere and find a little factory where we'd sit down and negotiate for hours. Over the two weeks we probably did about ten factories"

"Where did you stay at night?"

"Well, we either slept on the train, or we slept in – well, the word is 'hotel' – but they were basic as basic, just a bed in a room. I remember one place and the sign said 'Hotel' and it said the equivalent of one pound or one pound fifty a night. When I came to pay they said 'No, it's two pound fifty for you, or three pounds,' so I said, 'What the hell you talking about?' and they said 'It's double for foreigners.' That's how it was. A bit chaotic but you had to put up with what was there, right up on the Russian border, where most of the wood was coming from. But I got some small village factories in the area started on making things for me and spent quite a few years after that finding different village manufacturers all over the north to make different products for me."

This became Vance's pattern of travel for the next several years with visits becoming longer, just travelling, eating, sleeping and negotiating in the vast forest-covered wilderness of North China.

He laughs at the memory. "I really used to think I was like that bloke Indiana Jones but instead of searching for great big emeralds, I was searching for wood and a modern-day kitchen product I could make out there. I'd be sat on the back of the train with my whisky bottle watching the rails and the snow going away behind me, smoking my cigarette and drinking my whisky. So I really did think I was Indiana Jones. I enjoyed it. It was a great kick. Often better than alcohol."

"Who looked after the business at home?"

"Oh I had good people who'd been with me since the beginning. We kept contact when possible and I was sending good stuff home from China for them to make up and sell."

"But over the couple of years you travelled developing this new source of supply, how often were you away from the business in England and for how long each trip?"

"Once I realised the prospects in China I was away a lot for anything between six weeks and six months but mostly, for seven or eight weeks at a time."

"So how did you control your business at home from China?"

"I found it easier to control things in England by being constantly on the telephone from China. What helped me was that all my life I've been in and out of prison – always. And I've always had a charge hanging up over my head for something that might send me back to jail. So I always make sure that my businesses can operate without me. If I don't then I haven't got a business. It's always been like this so when I wasn't in prison I've always been able to go off anywhere in the world and explore and find something new and know things in England will be ok. And you have more time to run your business when travelling because at home the 'phone rings every five minutes putting all those problems on you. When travelling in those couple of years I had lots of time to think about what to do next, and make decisions. So running the business at home was quite easy, really."

"But how did you know that with you away and not looking over people's shoulders your day-to-day instructions were being properly followed?"

"Well, now, looking back, I'm sure things weren't being done a hundred per cent but at the time, with the advantages we had because of what I was buying cheap in China, eighty per cent was good enough. But now in two thousand and eight and nine, in this recession time, I have to jump in and make sure I keep close control whether at home or away because I can't afford to waste that twenty percent any longer. If I were trying to do all that control now it would be a damned sight harder than when I did it then."

"And how did you keep control of all these manufacturers at that time while you are travelling and bringing money into China to pay for the goods you're buying. How did you control shipping and quality?"

"Shipping was easy. You just booked a container, loaded it up and sent it home. But I sorted quality out a bit later after I learnt that if I didn't put my own quality control guy in their factories, I ended up with a pile of shit."

"A Chinese quality controller?"

"Yeah."

"And you could trust him to work for you and not try to help the Chinese producer?"

"Yeah. I paid him double what he could possibly earn doing the same job anywhere else. A factory might offer him a backhander but he knew his job wouldn't last if he took it and knew he was on a ridiculously good wicket with me. I'm paying him thirty-five quid a week. In any other job he'd be lucky to get fifteen quid a week and he's not going to let my thirty-five go. So he'd think, 'If I let anything bad go in that box, I'll never get this wage anywhere else.'"

"So the system worked?

" Yeah. But before that I had problems. I remember the first factory I got to make a kitchen cabinet. I told them every piece of wood has to be edged smooth all the way round. I don't want any bare rough side; I want it edged all the way round. They said, OK, we'll edge it all the way round. So when I went to inspect the first couple of containers they'd put this beautiful – absolutely beautiful – round edging on every piece of wood. Every single fookin' piece!"

"Isn't that what you asked for?"

"Yeah but these bits of wood are supposed to slot together. You can't put two bits of wood together with two rounded sides. So for me it was like, 'What on *earth* is this all about?' And remember, at that time two containers was a lot of money for me."

Vance laughs and spreads his hands, "You know what they said?' – he imitates a squeaky Chinese accent – 'But you tell us you want everything edging round.'"

He slaps his forehead. "No I didn't say 'Round 'I said, '*Around*' so they had to start again. They had to shave all these beautiful edges off."

"Did it cost you any more money?"

"It didn't cost me any more money but I had a shittier product because by the time they'd shaved all the edges off and they'd re-handled it I had a bag of shit. But in the end it worked because what I had was a solid wood kitchen cabinet. At least that's what I called it because it was a solid wood cabinet glued together although that description gave me trouble later."

Despite such early problems, Vance found completely virgin business territory without, at first, realising the long-term value of his discovery. Most factories in the forests worked wood in simple ways using antiquated machinery. During a series of visits with Mr Lee over the next two years, Vance set up a range of village manufacturing operations of considerable value to both sides. He found willing and happy workers able to follow designs exactly; the villagers found a guaranteed market plus access to capital and equipment, previously beyond their imaginings. The deals became almost perfect partnerships. But were they difficult to negotiate in a country creaking under the weight of communist bureaucracy?

"Not really. Mr Lee helped a lot. He'd worked for years with a company in the Harbin wood market but after a short time left them and started to work for me. He still does. He knows the way round all sorts of problems in China and he is now our wood expert, travelling round China and Russia. He's our contact with governments and we rely on him a lot. He's the man who knows everything about wood; where it comes from in Russia, where to dry it, where to sell it and he's as valuable today as he was at the beginning."

Vance started with a few villages copying the samples he'd brought. "They didn't know what they were making. They just copied these bits of wood that came in a box and their attitude was, 'God knows what it is but that's what he's asked us for so we'll get on with it.'"

"And they managed on their old machinery?"

"Not really. What they had was prehistoric so we soon began to send a lot of the machinery out ourselves."

"Did you donate it or sell it?"

"A bit of both. For some companies you'd donate the machinery, for some you'd sell it and others you'd set up in joint ventures. In the smaller villages, for instance, if one guy had a couple of grand of equipment he'd value it at half a million. So you'd say, OK if I come up with another half million pounds of machinery and a bit of cash I'm half in, am I?

"He'd say 'Yeah,' so, in England I'd go to the auctions or find bankrupt stock and buy machinery with a normal market value of around three or four hundred grand that probably cost me ten or twenty grand. I'd ship that out to China and throw in a bit of kick-start cash for raw materials and off I'd be with a joint venture. One thing led to another and I started dealing with up to a dozen different small village factories in the forests."

"And do the Chinese government, either local or national, know you're doing this?"

"Well, you're dealing with the local government in most places."

"And when you visit, do these officials come out and honour you?"

"Oh, God, yeah. It's come to the stage where I have to say no to going out boozing and eating. At the beginning I'd go out to every invitation and they'd be getting you pissed, wouldn't they, it'd be 'Gambi-gambi' – you know – down it in one and all this crap. But really they were licking your arse, weren't they? But now I just say, no – I'm not coming out drinking. Nope. Sorry. I've got to move on to the next town."

"It sounds as though you were really honoured."

"Oh yeah. When I arrive the mayor comes out and they put

up flags and the police and local soldiers are there and a band and a crowd of people clapping and waving and all sorts in most places."

"Somewhat different to England."

Vance sighs and rubs his face. "Oh yeah. A huge difference to England."

Vance's entrepreneurial approach, so new to China, worked well for both sides. But how did Vance go about starting such discussions in unfamiliar places so far from home and in a strange language?

I ask, "Did you walk into a village, see the local operation and like the people and begin by buying from them? Did you inspect what they already manufactured and think they'd do a job for you and that the best, or only, way was to become a partner?"

Vance chuckles. "You must remember that at that time in the whole of China there was not many white men and right up in the north there was absolute zero. I was absolutely unique and all the Chinese locals wanted to co-operate. And I suppose, the word went round that the Englishman's come in to town. So they weren't the hardest people to negotiate with. But you first of all start buying simple things like shelves off them. Then if they needed certain machines to make parts of the door or the cabinet you'd have to supply the machine. But at first, the main reason I went to the forest was because they had the wood. The rest came later."

"Remind me in which year this happened?"

Vance frowns, trying to remember. "Two thousand or two thousand-and-one. Oh God, how things have moved. No. It was two thousand and then once I'd sorted out my wood supply, wooden doors, wooden cabinets, etc., then I had something unique in Britain, I had a real wood, a solid wood kitchen cabinet."

"How long did it take you to reach that stage?"

"Six months."

"Was that six months as one visit or over several visits?"

"Six months over two or three visits. In that time I had working in wood all done and dusted. So once I'd sorted out my kitchen cabinets it was a case of developing other products in the kitchen industry."

"Such as?"

Vance becomes excited at the memory, reliving his multiple adventures; his eyes light up and his voice rises, "Well, I travelled from one side of China to the other visiting big factories that made fridges and found they'd never heard of an integrated fridge/ freezer built into a kitchen. So I bought samples in England and sent them out to these big companies and say, 'Copy that,' and they'd say, 'But this is very technical, how do we do this or how do we do that?' and I'd say, 'You're the experts. I don't know the answers to your questions. You've got the sample so copy it like *that!* Exact! As you see it.' So they did and I was the first man ever to build an integrated fridge/freezer in China. Then I was the first to build a dishwasher in China."

At this point Vance began to realise the rich possibilities of what he had started and began copying every kitchen product he could think of, from dishwashers, fridges and freezers to ovens, hobs, extractors; buying the best possible in Britain and sending it for exact replication in China.

He said, "When I realised I could get into the electronics side of it, not just the woodwork and cheap handles and hinges but the dishwashers, ovens and all, I made a big jump. That was when I saw I had real value here although it often involved me paying for all the tooling costs. These could run into tens and tens of thousands, but the tooling to make, say, a fridge, in Britain could run into a million pounds or more. This was when I began to think I should build things in China. Not just *buy* things but really *build* things – my own factories perhaps – and have a proper future in that country."

"So you would find a factory and agree to set it up with tooling to make your product. I imagine they were happy with that."

"Yeah. But sometimes it wasn't that simple. For instance – a dishwasher – something never even been heard of in China before me. So where can I get a dishwasher made? What I did was go to washing machine factories and tell 'em: 'Your washing machine is nearly there but to make a dishwasher we just need to change a few things. Instead of it going round that way I want it going round this way etc, etc.'"

"How did they take to that?"

"Well, it was before all the big white goods people from Europe moved in to China so the Chinese all wanted to be part of me. They were very keen on this new idea and they'd say, 'Yeah, yeah, yeah. We'll make it for you.' It was again, hey – the white man's coming to town and I want to work with him. And they did it to the extent that I'd be visiting, say, the Chinese equivalent of Panasonic and driving in to their town at midnight and the whole board of directors would come out to welcome me and we'd have a meeting at one in the morning, if I wanted it, or any time I was ready, with all the managing directors and the full board."

"And were these biggish companies?"

"Some were big and some were small."

"But even with the big ones, you paid for the tooling?"

"Yeah. Then signed contracts so they were not allowed to manufacture those products for anybody else in Europe, nor allowed to use my tooling for any similar product. By the time the big boys in England got to China, Vance Miller had stitched the factories up so they couldn't manufacture for anyone else without my permission. So a lot of the big boys are buying my product from China with no fookin' idea I'm getting two-and-a-half percent commission from these factories they're dealing with."

"Can I put that in the book?"

"Yeah, of course you can because they all closed the doors on me."

"Who?"

"All the big retailers in England. When at first everything I bought was being manufactured in Europe and I was getting a name for myself in England they tried to stop me by telling manufacturers not to deal with me. When I went to the European manufacturers the door would be closed and they'd say, 'Sorry we've already heard of you and been told we can't deal with you.' They were being told this by some of the big British companies that I now supply with appliances and things. All the big retailers put the boot in. Stop him! You're not supplying him! If you do we won't buy from you. End of story."

"Then you turned the tables?"

"Yeah. I thought, fook you then. If you won't make my products in Europe I'll go to China and make my own. So I went out there and developed all this stuff and now, as I say, when people get out there they have to buy my products often without knowing it."

But the real value to China of Vance and his risk-taking business approach shows best among the sparse population in the northern forests, along the Russian border. Many small villages, previously with little or no work now hum with activity, turning out doors, shelving and cabinets for Vance's fast-expanding kitchen business.

I ask, "How many people did you employ or have working for you at the beginning?"

"Just one. Mr Lee. Well, two, if you include me."

"I mean how many once you'd started giving work to people with no real chance of employment before you came along."

Vance frowns, considering the question and how to reply.

"All I can say is from day one it was nothing. But now – today – the number of people employed directly or directly working to supply me is…thousands."

He pauses to savour the word and repeats, "Thousands," with a shake of his head and a grin at the wonder of it all.

## Chapter Eight
# *Buying Cheap In China –*
# *The Entrepreneur*

Vance spent the next couple of years rushing around China discovering and setting up manufacturers for his kitchen products.

Over twenty-four hectic months and thousands of miles he listened and learnt, adding detailed study of Chinese manufacturing and costs to his home market expertise. Increasingly he bought at keen prices far below European terms, whilst ensuring the Chinese factory made profit.

Vance laughs and says, "Between us, Mr Lee and me learned almost everything there is to know about buying kitchen parts in China long before all those fat cats in England got off their arses and came no farther than the big cities to try and catch up."

Most suppliers, large and small, seemed incredibly willing to cooperate and supply, although some – very few – dropped out or were abandoned when faced with Vance's vigorous approach to price and quality negotiation.

Eventually he found those long, hard visits to places in the middle of nowhere, sleeping rough in trains, sheds and terrible hotels, beginning to pay off. Using buying and negotiating skills, honed and sharpened in the crucible of China, his delivered price to Britain came right down and pushed his UK kitchen sales higher and higher.

The fascinating documentary made by Alastair Cook for Channel 4 Television, *Brits Get Rich In China*, followed Vance for several weeks on buying expeditions. During the programme Vance tells the interviewer, "I travelled to Inner Mongolia and Tibet, up into mountains and through jungles and down mines. I've been everywhere. I've got to go right to where it begins life. I'm not going to deal through no middleman. I'm not going to buy through no wholesaler. How can I get it cheaper like that? If I want a kitchen I chop down a tree."

The Mill began to fill with Vance's special quality selling points – cabinets, doors and shelving made from real wood – plus granite worktops built into a kitchen that undercut competition prices by up to a hundred per cent. Vance found that his need for good granite turned him and his business in an entirely different direction, until finally – "I bought a quarry."

The same BBC documentary shows Vance arguing with a Chinese granite producer over quality. The supplier, deep among mountains in rural China, took Vance a couple of years to find.

Too cute to be taken in by the smart-arse quarry owner, Vance refuses to inspect granite worktops from cases neatly packed ready for shipment and placed in a prominent position.

In the documentary Vance stands on a case of granite, waving his arms and shouting, "This case here is so, so, *so* inviting to have a look in because it sticks out and says open me, open me, open me so I'm not going to open it. They're so clever these Chinese guys. This one is purposely sticking out and they're sure I'll pick it but I'm not going to pick it. I'll go for the one that'll probably be the last they expect me to pick out."

There follows a quite hilarious episode when the argument runs on and on so Mr Wang – to waste time and tire Vance out – sends his men off for a break suggesting Vance goes too. Vance bellows his refusal to leave insisting that hidden cases are brought out and opened while he watches. The charade continues for a couple of hours while Mr Wang tries a three-card-trick shuffle with the imperfect samples. Day turns to night but Vance still refuses to be ushered away, sticking with grim resolve to absolute insistence that the cases he wants to examine are opened.

Eventually, Vance wins. Wang surrenders and Vance's chosen cases produce granite worktops marked with a web of scars. Vance rubs his finger over the damaged surfaces. "Look at all these wheel marks," he says. "It's all scratched here."

Mr Wang blandly suggests you can't see the marks in daylight. Vance snarls, "Oh yeah? What will trading standards inspectors say when I come out with that excuse eh? And what do I tell my customer? 'Get a night shift job Mrs Jones so you'll be in bed and don't see the scratches on your kitchen top in daytime!'"

He claps a hand to his forehead and shouts to camera, "These guys are treating me as if I'm some arsehole from MFI just cruised in off a banana boat; as if I've just stepped out of my five star hotel with a hangover. Last thing they want to do is stroll around this dirty old yard in their Armani suits and Gucci shoes. This is the last place they want to be isn't it?" Vance turns and snaps at Mr Wang, "Well, unfortunately, pal, you've got fookin' Mr Scumbag from Rochdale here who doesn't give a toss about the shit around him in a place like this."

How the interpreter can translate such broad Lancashire is not clear but Vance's loud and direct style makes him successful in buying from China. He digs deep into the country, travelling for months at a time, negotiating, arguing; squeezing suppliers into deals he *knows* they can reach by demonstrating detailed knowledge of international pricing and kitchen manufacture. In the end most manufacturers give way and agree terms, beaten down by Vance's forceful approach but benefiting from huge orders and long production runs.

Vance then follows up personally, returning constantly, checking quality of production and finished product before shipment. In this way he earns respect and fear, forcing high-class kitchen parts from the Chinese by his assertive confident manner.

The documentary follows Vance on a buying trip to what is known as 'Tap City'. He is driving south from Shanghai, swaying and singing to loud music blaring from his DVD player. A voiceover explains that dirt-cheap materials and wages of only twenty pence an hour have transformed China into a giant factory supplying a world market with insatiable appetite for their rock-bottom prices.

Whole cities have turned into one-product centres known by the name of the item they manufacture. Vance's journey takes him past Condom City, Zip City and Bra City on his way to Tap City where most of the three million inhabitants make taps. He is visiting a salesman called Black Horse, the Chinese version of Black Sheep, so named because he undercuts everyone else in the tap industry.

But for this visit Black Horse is not cutting price. He is hoping to sell Vance a new design of shower tap costing almost one hundred RMB yuan. The negotiation runs back and forth with Vance and Black Horse arguing hard both for money and

– so says the documentary voiceover – for national pride; East facing West in a high decibel contest.

Black Horse starts by showing a tap of lower quality and receives a response straight from Oldham. Vance slaps the item back into Black Horse's hand, saying, "Shove that up your arse. I'll not be talked into accepting an inferior bastard product." He points to the new design. "I want this one."

Vance has no doubt he could sell the quality tap for many times the Chinese asking price in Britain but is programmed never to accept first offer. So he shouts and argues and starts dismantling the tap.

Waving two components in the air he barks, "Right. Come on. How much do these cost?" and answers his own question with a triumphant, "*Nothing*! So two times nothing is fookin' nothing."

Twirling a shining chrome pipe only inches from Black Horse's nose, Vance asks, "And how much is *that*?"

Black Horse fiddles at his calculator, muttering "This is my lowest price," but you can see he is wilting Vance whispers, "Mind your fingers don't slip," and the interpreter says, "Three point five."

Vance laughs and says, "You didn't think cheeky Englishman would know what the price should be. You thought he'd just say

OK, no problem, I accept."

The negotiation ends abruptly. Both sides seem happy. Vance steps forward and this little spat ends with smiles, a bow and a handshake. Vance grins into camera and says, "Dropped from ninety-four to fifty-four and a half. Great. At home I'll be able to sell those at nine pounds forty all day long and no other bastard will be able to come here and get a better price, 'cos I sat here all day and argued for the damned thing."

Who won? Did Black Horse have a fallback price he never reached? Did Vance have a prepared upper limit he may have gone to? We'll never know but both sides probably met in the middle, in the way of good businessmen. And they parted on good terms with Vance commissioning Black Horse to the manufacture of several million taps.

# Chapter Nine
## *Making It In China –*
## *The International Businessman*

By the end of two years hard and sometimes dangerous travel, Vance found himself with over a hundred suppliers spread across China; some good, some unreliable. So he acquired land and started construction of a factory near Harbin to manufacture his own doors, cupboards and kitchen carcases. At the same time he began planning a large warehouse in Guangzhou in the south to gather and ship the enormous amount of kitchen equipment he now bought.

These brave moves – the action of an entrepreneur willing to take unusual and enormous risk – heralded Vance's change from buying-and-selling trader to international businessman, responsible for building, owning and managing factories through staff controlled and trained to his methods.

Losing his temper over Mr Wang's casual attitude to the quality of his marble slabs might have been decisive in this shift although I doubt Vance realised it at the time.

I ask, "Did you buy Wang's granite quarry?"

"No. It came over like that on television but he didn't own a quarry. He was a trader buying in blocks and making worktops. But I'd been getting fooked about for so long and so often by Wang and others like him I decided that this was the end. I couldn't get anyone to finish worktops properly. They just didn't care; they really didn't, so I had no alternative than to buy a quarry."

"How did you go about that?"

"Simply talked to people in local government with authority to sell me a chunk of land. That's all a quarry is, just a big chunk of land. You can buy a chunk of land that's three or four acres in area but goes twenty acres down."

"And was the quarry you bought already working?"

"No. It wasn't being used."

"So you went to local government and said you wanted to manufacture your own granite slabs?"

"Yeah."

"And they're going to be interested because…"

"Employment," says Vance. "They were interested in reopening the quarry for local employment."

"How many people?"

"In the quarry? About a hundred."

The documentary shows Vance inspecting his new purchase.

A deep wide rocky hole, of course, but lined with shaky wooden steps held together by quivering poles. Even the brave Vance, veteran of US jails and African revolutions needs all his steely nerves to hang on and creep to the bottom.

But Vance's brand of almost Victorian entrepreneurship works. Ignoring the rich city and coastal areas, he travels deep into the empty centre and north of this vast country where millions of people scratch a bare existence. The Victorians brought religion and trade. Vance brings money, machinery and work.

The documentary ends with Vance climbing into his special bus with a cheery wave to camera as he sets off on a five-day journey to Inner Mongolia to buy a forest.

"To buy a forest?" I ask.

"Yes. I bought an oak forest. I asked my men to find me something that's for sale so they did and I went and bought it."

Vance throws his hands in the air. His mind flicks back in time and he becomes agitated. His voice rises and he snaps, "Look, I'm pissed off at having to rely on dud suppliers and getting cheated and getting a load of logs that's all rotten in the middle and it's just like, hey, I can't deal with this shit any longer. I need to decide what's coming into my factory so, again, same as the quarry, you need to get involved in your own forest."

"So it was the same sequence of events? Somebody found

you something for sale then you went and spoke to the local government and purchased the land with standing wood?"

"Yeah."

"And this was at the same time as buying land, building two factories, buying a quarry and purchasing an enormous amount of manufactured goods from suppliers all over China?"

"Yeah."

"Was this rush of investment around the same period of time?"

"Yeah."

"How on earth did you finance it all?"

"I was turning over big money in England – between fifty and eighty thousand a week – that I used to buy from Chinese suppliers."

"So you had enough margin in your cash flow to cover all running costs for both the buying in China and the selling in England?"

"Yeah, and Barclays in England lent me one point one million pounds against The Mill to finance the rest. They gave me a five year loan but took the bastard back after one year and closed my account."

"Why?

"I don't know. Perhaps *you* can ask 'em."

"Perhaps later. For now I want to stick to your operation in

China. What size of forest did you buy?"

"Six thousand acres and we replant absolutely everything. As we're going along we replant the lot."

"Without the replanting, how many years of wood do you estimate you had at the time you bought the forest?"

"Oh, the rest of my life."

"And how many people do you employ there?"

"I haven't taken full advantage of the forest so not many. I could be selling wood to other manufacturers but I'm not. I may at some point but at present I'm just using it for myself. I would say that in the forest I probably have about fifty people."

"So, in China you own a granite quarry and a forest and two factories and you're supplying your own companies in England and as I understand it, you're now supplying kitchen retailers and manufacturers in the local China market from the two factories. In addition you are setting up a retail chain in China to sell your kitchens. How did that start? You bought the factories first?"

"I *built* the factories first. I bought land and built the factories, one in the south in Guangzhou, the other up north near Harbin. I've got photographs of all the stages. The factory in the north was to be built in four stages and we've completed two-and-a-half stages up to now."

"The stages being parts of manufacturing units so the first

stage gives you, doors, for instance and the next stage is for, say, kitchen carcases?"

"Yeah. That is the Harbin factory; the Guangzhou building is completely finished but in Harbin we have more space than we actually need just now."

"Is that factory space or land space?"

"Both. Finished factory space and extra land to carry on building later."

"And what do you precisely produce?"

"In Guangzhou we manufacture handles and taps and it's also used as our warehouse for distributing products throughout the world. We'll exhibit in, say, Russia or China or other countries and then we'll send mixed containers from our Guangzhou warehouse."

"And what do you produce in the Harbin factory?"

"Kitchen cabinets, doors, cornice and pelmet, all the trimmings, etc; injection mouldings, all the plastics…"

"And in all these cases you bought the machinery and sent it to China?"

"Yeah. But not all from England, some was manufactured brand spanking new in China. We take an old knackered machine out to China and say, 'Copy that, brand new,' and they do. The rest we bought from bankrupt factories in places like Germany and Italy as well as England."

"Factories made bankrupt by Chinese competition?"

"Yeah. Funny isn't it? You know what makes the difference and causes those bankruptcies? A machine that costs one hundred and sixty thousand pounds in England costs six grand to make in China."

The Channel 4 *Brits Get Rich In China* documentary shows Vance examining machinery in his factory. He points out two large German made machines and says to camera, "These are presses for coating vinyl on cabinet doors. There's about a million pounds in them two machines. I bought them from a bankruptcy back in England for about fifteen grand each."

He strolls past two other machines and says, "These put all the holes in the cabinets. Believe it or not – I'm not lying –these were twenty quid a piece from an auction."

Shaking his head he repeats in a tone of incredulity, "*Twenty quid a piece*"

He shrugged. " Nobody wants to produce in England any more."

Here we see a brilliant entrepreneur breaking from his chrysalis and becoming an international businessman – perhaps without yet realising it.

I ask, "And in these two factories, how many people do you

currently employ?

"About three-hundred-and-fifty in the Harbin factory and down in Guangzhou – it's more of a warehouse than a factory – I've only got about twenty or thirty people working in the warehouse but there's sales people connected to it and drivers etc, so there's probably about a hundred-and-fifty altogether in Guangzhou."

"Then, after completion of the factories you decided to expand by setting up a chain of kitchen retail stores throughout China. I believe you now have around a hundred stores. Did this sideways development into retail come from business planning or because you had all that product rolling out of your new factories and thought, hell, I ought to be selling it retail?"

"I had all the stock on the ground in China and as far as I was concerned I was the kitchen expert of the world. All my kitchen products were being made in China to European specifications and branded with European names and all of a sudden I saw a massive expansion of European companies exporting Western style kitchens to China and selling on the retail market. So I thought 'Wow! What's happening here, mate?'"

"And you decided to have a go at them?"

"Yeah. Here are these German manufacturers exporting from Europe when I'm already manufacturing that same product here in China. I don't have to pay European wages *and* pay to export the bastard to China *and* pay huge import duties. Hell! I'm already here so I thought *I'm* going to start retailing kitchens from my own retail stores."

"So it was not business planning, it was an entrepreneurial approach. You just couldn't resist the lure of another big chance – perhaps a big gamble – could you? How many stores did you start with?"

"Well… um… none! As you say, I didn't really plan it. I just started with one and kept going until I got to a hundred."

"And how did you finance this? From cash flow and profit or through a bank?"

"The money I was making in England and China paid for it and my loan from Barclays paid for it. I never have any spare money as capital. I'm always skint because I'm always developing."

"So it was a decision you made overnight and just got started."

"Yeah."

"In other words, you were simply being Vance."

"Yeah."

"And is this move into retail stores *very* successful or just successful?"

Vance pauses, frowns and makes a low groaning sound deep in his throat. "Not successful. I find that one hundred showrooms later a lot of the investments I made, like a warehouse set-up for supplying my showrooms in China, is a bag of shit."

"Why?"

"Why? Because China's not what we think it is. They're not ready yet. They haven't got the money to spend."

"Are we talking about the retail business?"

"Yeah. We're talking about my retail operation in China and people in general. I'm not talking about the factories. They're fantastic. But the retail is horrendous. It's not worth the effort." Vance threw his head back and groaned again.

"So are you going to pull out of it?"

"Yeah. I'm thinking of pulling out of retail in China. But I'm not the only one who's made a mistake. China's covered in tens of thousands of apartment blocks all completely empty. Everybody thought that China was ready to move into the Western world style of living but it's not."

"Why did you go into retail when it is not really your line of business?"

"Let me explain where I went wrong big time – big bad decision – a big bad mistake. I got carried away with what was happening in China. I saw it as a slow market because of the lack of money but thought that in less than ten years time China would be just like America. By then I reckoned people will all be driving cars, they'll all have jobs and they'll all have lots of money and I'd have two-thousand stores all over China all making big money. I thought that if I set up all over the country during the next five years, nobody else would be able to move in. I'll have it all sewn up. Nobody will be able to enter the kitchen market because I opened my stores when it cost between five hundred and a thousand pounds a store. When China becomes the new America, no one else will get a chance. They'll have to pay fifty to sixty grand to open a store."

Vance sits down and stares at the wall, silent for a moment, his mind obviously far away in China studying a broken dream.

I hate to break in but ask, "And how are you going to fold it down?"

"Well, a lot of money and effort went into building up that retail and it's a bitter pill to swallow."

I try and cheer him up by saying, "But it's a clever decision to pull out early if you can see it's not working."

"Failure is horrible and still a bitter pill but I'm getting a lot of business being thrown at me from Ireland. I can immediately just swallow the pill, and move stock from the Chinese retail stores into Ireland and have another go there."

"Retail or wholesale?"

"Both. I've found some really rich Irish guys who want to go into business with me but I want to do it on my own. I've found a nice big warehouse right in the centre of Ireland and I've got to make a big decision. Do I go it alone or do I go in with these guys who have a lot of money?"

I hold up a hand and stop Vance from saying more. "That's for another Chapter. We need to stay talking about China so let's go to the export business you mentioned earlier. I think you're exporting from China to… did you mention Russia?"

"We're exporting to countries all over the world."

"Do you have agents or your own people in these countries?"

"We don't have anything. We just have customers who buy our products. Before I set up if anyone wanted to buy, say, hinges or taps or whatever, they had to buy full container loads. That was the way it was done – a full container of one product or nothing. But we've changed that and become supply specialists and when we exhibit internationally we show that if you want to go and buy a full container of hinges or taps or handles or sinks from somebody in China then go and do it. But not many people, not even the big boys like me or MFI or B&Q, can afford to buy full containers of handles or hinges or taps or anything else. We're specialists in supplying the kitchen industry, so if you want, buy a container with some handles in it, hinges in it, or taps, dishwashers, fridges, cabinets and sinks…"

"A mixture in one container?"

"Yeah. You can have a mixed container from us, worth, say, forty grand. Otherwise you could lay out forty grand just to get a load of hinges but why do that when from us you can get the whole mixture without any problem?"

"So effectively, you can ship thirty kitchens in parts rather than a million hinges."

"Yeah."

"So the customers in these other countries are the likes of B&Q and Magnet and so on in England?"

"Well, you might have some large independents and even some smaller companies. You get a lot of smaller people going to China with fifty grand in their pocket and that's all they've got and they're looking for an opportunity. We can help them in a way no one else can"

"Is it true to say that within a fairly short time, the business in China – and from China - will really dwarf your UK business?"

"It already dwarfs the UK business. The international business – sending containers here there and everywhere – is the main one."

"Bigger than anything else you do including the UK?"

"Yes. Exporting from China is almost twice the turnover of what I do in England. Profit margin is less but running expenses are next to nowt. So if I sell, say five-hundred dishwashers from China, the margin per dishwasher is only twelve percent but with no other costs the end profit is much larger per dishwasher than in England."

"So the cash flow gives greater benefit because you keep more of it."

"Yeah. I just load a container and off it goes. Goodbye container out and hello money in. I'm selling to Russia, Dubai, England and Japan and even to Kazakhstan. I sell to America too but they're not doing so well right now."

"So you have a pretty wide-ranging international business."

"Yeah. I'm doing things all over the world and you know the bullshit problems I get in this country? Well I don't get anything like it in any other country."

"You mean none of the extreme personal and business pressure from legal authorities and press and television here at home?"

"Right! In other countries I'm honoured, not shat upon like in England. But to bring in a glossy note, I've just got an order from the British Government for five thousand kitchens and they don't even know they're buying from me. It's brilliant…"

"You're selling to the British Government?"

"Well, to a big company that maintains and rebuilds properties for the Government and local authorities. They're one of the biggest building companies in England but I'd never heard of them until they met us at the Shanghai exhibition and after that I got talking on the telephone to this guy, Dave, who organises things for them in China. He lives in China on the other side of the country to where I am and he sends one of his inspectors up to see our Harbin factory because they're a proper professional company. The inspector says, 'Fantastic factory,' and sent me an inspection report. I'll give it you for the book. It says this factory is beautiful, wonderful and definitely one we should deal with. Well Dave wants to do a deal with me and on the 'phone he's calling me Paul."

"Paul?"

"I don't want to call myself Vance, so for this deal I'm Paul 'cos it's an English company and I don't want to be Vance 'cos everyone knows about me and they say 'Ooh, hey, I know you. You've been on the telly…' So this guy Dave says to me, 'I got a description of you from my factory inspector and I know you're heavily into kitchens and all that but you know, before we were sent to start sourcing from the Chinese market we were shown videos about China as a learning tool. One of those videos was a programme called *Brits Get Rich In China*, and he said, 'Are you *really* called Paul? Or are you Vance?' so I had to say, 'No I'm not called Paul. I'm Vance.'"

"Aha! You were rumbled."

"Yeah, rumbled. But after a moment of thinking he said, 'Well I thought so but let's keep that between me and you.'"

Vance rolls back in his chair, laughing and shaking his head.

I ask, "Can I put that in the book?"

Vance nods and grins, savouring the moment and repeats, "Well let's keep that between me and you…"

"What happened next?"

"He bought five thousand kitchens for two and a half million dollars. That was two hundred and fifty quid a kitchen with the exchange rate at that time."

"And you can do it at that price?"

"Yeah. The margin's tight but you know what? He sent a report saying your product's too good. I'll give you a copy for the book. Can you imagine that? Your product is too good. Your specification is too high. Lower it."

"Did you drop your price on the lower specification?"

"No, I kept my price because I told him I wasn't willing to lower my standards. I didn't want to supply something I know is inferior. I know how to build the perfect product so why are you asking me to supply a quality less than that? He said, 'Cos that's what we're used to from our English supplier. All I want you to do is meet their spec.' "

"So did you lower your specification?"

"Only slightly but I kept the price because the lower quality gave me more manufacturing waste but it was still a better quality than he was getting in England. It was a massively tight deal for me. Massively tight."

"Was it worth it?"

"Well, there was only twenty per cent in it and I think fook it, should I do the deal? Shall I put up with all this aggravation and manufacturing problems and shipping to England for so little profit? Then I think, hang on, it'll only take me ten weeks to complete the order and it's half a million dollars profit – that's two hundred and fifty grand sterling. Luckily the pound's gone down so it's now three hundred grand sterling."

"And that's money you can use."

"Of course. It covers the cost of running the factory."

"So this direct international business is worth far more effort than messing about with retail outlets."

"Too right. Every week there's a kitchen exhibition somewhere in the world. I can send my team from China to exhibit, take them big orders and look after the customers."

"With such a big international business in China are your accounts consolidated so your UK operation and accounts include the Chinese operation?"

"No. Totally different businesses – they're registered as individual companies in China and England."

"So your accounts in China show a completely separate cost and profit centre?"

"Yeah. And the good thing is that when you open a new business in China you get three years tax-free."

"So the retail outlets are set up in a new company that gets the three years benefit?"

"Yeah. My three years are just coming to an end on the factories but the retail shops are a new business so I've started a new three years with those but I'm still going to close the buggers down."

"Who looks after your accounts and legal work in China?"

"I've got a Chinese accountant in-house and a fulltime solicitor to deal with all the bullshit that China has to throw at me. I need them because there's a tax for everything in China – they invent taxes as they go along. They've even got a tax on noise but it's not really a tax, it's part of a game between you and the man trying to collect the tax. And it's all about backhanders, it's bullshit, it's crap. The taxmen try to invent problems in China so they can help you cure them for twenty-five percent of the price of doing it legally."

It is now late at night and we've been talking for several hours. The telephone rings and Vance starts a long conversation with one of his British staff in China. I have time to sit back and think through how this man – a self-described poorly educated ex-criminal – came to such success in a foreign and quite alien country.

Then I remember scenes of the *Brits Get Rich In China* documentary showing Vance using his originality and daring to beat strict Chinese rules banning foreigners travelling throughout rural China. Who else would have found such an intelligent way round such annoyance? Vance simply bought a huge new bus, fitted it out with luxury bedrooms, kitchen, lounge and office and painted the whole thing in bright colours and Olympic logos proclaiming 'Olympic Inspection Committee' in Chinese and English.

He says, "It's illegal but if we get stopped by the police we just tell 'em we're the Olympic inspection committee here to check your grounds and whatnot."

Vance acts out a frightened Chinese policeman raising his hands and thinking, 'Shit. I'm not going to lose China the Olympics for one simple argument' and waving Vance through, saying, "Ok, Pal, off you go."

Vance says "And the bus makes life a lot more comfortable doesn't it? Because when you get into these remote places things are pretty horrendous."

"But how will you travel now the Olympics are over?"

"My situation is changed. I've no need to travel in the same way but if I have to again I'll find a way."

The end of the documentary shows Vance setting off in his bus on a three-day trip to buy his forest and reading the ancient Chinese classic *The Art Of War* now used, says the voiceover, by modern Chinese tycoons to plan their business strategies.

It may be such attention to detail that spurs Vance to success in China. Or it may be his complex blend of Lancashire grit, speed of thought and absolute self-confidence. He seems to see everything as fun and adventure and, as the documentary says, he probably looks upon China as a giant playground.

He certainly seems to have the knack, skill and open-minded approach to take the right risks and decisions to come out the winner in China.

This same combination of qualities may be helping him survive nine years of continual media, official and legal; attacks on his reputation and business in Britain.

# Chapter Ten
## *Beating The Competition – Business According To Vance*

How did Vance build a small, stuttering, low quality operation into the third largest kitchens supplier in Britain over only eight years?

Such expansion whilst under the continual extreme legal and media pressure Vance suffered may be unprecedented. At the same time he saw off all competition, both direct and underhand, as he describes it, by turning kitchen marketing on its head with high quality granite tops and real wood kitchens at lower prices than competitors' heavily promoted best offerings for chipboard kitchens.

Once Vance bought The Mill he needed it filled with product. His newfound skill in sourcing and buying from China gave him a flood of quality kitchens at prices so attractive his business expanded at enormous speed. Building his wholly owned factories in China increased the flow of saleable kitchen products even more.

Until now my conversations with Vance concentrated on the dramas of his early criminal days and his amazing ability to recognise China as an important product source long before competitors even realised that country existed as a supplier. Now I need to discover what strength of mind and determination smashed through barriers likely to daunt and demolish a possibly more conventional personality.

I finally get Vance to break a busy spell of work and court appearances in Britain plus trips to China and sit with me in a hotel room. He is tired and in pain from a twisted spinal disc and, to begin with, not happy at being interrogated again.

He lies on the bed to ease his pain and glares at me so I start by saying, "Vance, what I need to know is how, once you got going in China and saw this flood of goods coming in and passing through The Mill, you went about building up the business in Britain almost from scratch?"

The question seems to puzzle Vance. He thinks hard, whispering to himself, "How did I build the business up from scratch from The Mill?" Frowning he clicks his tongue against his gums in a popping sound before asking, "Sorry…what was the question? How did I build the business up from The Mill? Well, um…once the products started coming in I just had to sell them, really, and deliver them didn't I? It was just a matter of more of everything. More advertising, more sales people, more office people, more services, more everything."

Frustrated at his reticence I almost snap at him when saying, "Yes. But Vance – there's more of a story than that. You can't just have a sudden rush of product into a relatively small business with big new premises to fill and use as a conduit. Both product and general expansion need finance and a structure to handle it all in the first place. You had to shift the stock through as sales by building up office staff, building up your sales force; building up advertising and distribution. So what was your thinking when this big opportunity with product presented itself from China?"

He frowns and thinks hard, obviously casting his mind back to plans and actions now probably forgotten. "Well…it was just a matter of pushing the real wood products. The fact that I could source and make my product out of real wood cheaper than anybody else could make out of chipboard and I could make solid granite worktops cheaper than anybody else could make chipboard worktops was what I had to push. So that's what I pushed."

"And that became the basis of your advertising?"

"Yes. We advertised on radio, in newspapers, television, magazines, we advertised wherever we could. And we set up a hundred and eighty trailers all along the motorways to advertise our quality kitchens at low prices. I did that by speaking to farmers and asking if we could put trailers in their fields. I think at one stage we were spending around a hundred and fifty thousand pounds a week on advertising. Some weeks we'd make a busy TV advertising week and spend a quarter of a million pounds, or something like that."

"And the business was able to stand such heavy expense even at such an early stage?"

"Yeah. The business grew fast and the fact that we had a real wood product and solid granite worktop just made the difference."

"But was it also important that you had your own dedicated source of supply?"

"Yeah, of course."

"And was this the time you decided to build your own factories in China?"

"At the beginning I had no intention of building a factory in China. But when we started buying what should have been superior products from China, we found quality varied from factory to factory. We needed standard quality but had no control, so decided it was easier to build our own factory where we could manufacture to our own standard and check and regulate product from other suppliers."

"So you decided to build at least one factory – although you ended up with several."

"We have two factories in the north where we manufacture and one down in the south where we just gather stuff together from suppliers and check quality before shipment."

"And how did you go about the selling in England?"

"We have salesmen who only go out after someone has made an initial inquiry."

"So you do no cold calling?"

"No. Customers phone us up and ask for a kitchen plan and we send out a salesman – a designer – to plan and draw a kitchen for them in their own house. But we don't chase people or call at your door or ring you up, bugging you and saying you've won a prize and things like that."

"It is interesting to think you can do a quarter of a million pounds advertising in a couple of weeks on television…"

"In a week," Vance interrupted. "We'd do that in a week."

"Sorry. In a week – but it's interesting to think the business would stand that expenditure at your low prices. But you're telling me that's how it was?"

"Well, we were selling a product that could have commanded a much better selling price than chipboard because it was wood and solid granite but we were buying it for less than the price of chipboard so sold for a lower price than the chipboard sold by our competitors."

This seemed to spur a revival of Vance's usual aggressive energy. The pain in his back apparently forgotten he hauled himself upright. His eyes hardened and I saw memories of those fighting days flood back.

His voice rose and he snapped, "Yeah. That was when Trading Standards realised they were fighting a real battle here. 'Hey, this man's got a huge, huge advantage on the market. How best to hurt him and let's attack his advantage.' So that's when they started to really go after us, saying, your solid wood's not real wood so I said, 'Ok we'll call it real wood,' and it all became bullshit, bullshit, bullshit from them. They needed to destroy my advantage but trying to stop me selling real wood kitchens and solid granite worktops was like trying to take my queen in a game of chess."

"But they never managed."

"No. They never managed."

"And they've been at it for eight years."

"Yeah."

"And how did your competitors, who probably never even saw you coming at first, react to all this?"

"Well, apart from going bust, nothing else really."

"So they didn't try to match your pricing?"

"Well, they can't get the product for a start…"

I break in, almost shouting Vance down to say, "Ah, that's the point. Let's go to that. Where did their product come from?"

He paused for a second then said, "British and European industry runs on sales of high turnover chipboard kitchens. Companies like B&Q and MFI and the people manufacturing big volumes of machine-made product are not geared up for wood. Their factories all churn out chipboard and MDF."

"Is that still the case now in 2009?"

"Yeah."

"So you're still outselling them?"

"Yeah."

"And who was it said that your operation pushed MFI into bankruptcy and out of business?"

"A few people have said it but not me. And there've been similar comments on the Internet but I'm quite sure it was not just my business that brought them down. It was also MFI's stupidity and naivety and the fact nobody in that organisation really knew their arse from their elbow."

"Naivety in what way?"

"Well, they didn't have one man running the company. There wasn't one man that went to bed each night thinking about the next move. There wasn't one man who cared whether MFI earned money next week or lost money next week. The management running the company killed that business. If I ran my company in the same way I'd be bankrupt as well. Management don't care. They only care about their salaries. They don't care about the business."

"And what about the other big people – I understand they all ganged up on you in trade shows?"

"Yeah. The other companies realised they couldn't compete with me so they started lobbying the Kitchen Associations that run the trade shows and doing everything they could to stop me from exhibiting. Even as far as when I'd booked a stand at an exhibition someone else would bid more money to buy my stand just to stop me getting in there. They did everything in their power. I think they realised my product was dangerous to them. They even ganged up and got the people who run Trade Shows to ban me from attending by threatening a boycott if I were allowed to book stands. They couldn't compete so they had to get up to all sorts of tricks to stop me."

"On another subject – you've never gone the way of the other big kitchen companies by having a chain of retail stores?"

"We're opening stores up slowly but I could never really afford a chain of retail stores. That's the reason I never went for them, plus the way we originally started our business was a cheap and easy way of selling kitchens."

"And is that still the case?"

"Yeah. Stores are expensive but at least now with the economic downturn you can choose your stores more easily. If you wanted a prime position two or three or four years ago they were hard to get, they were all taken up and nobody was letting go. Now all of a sudden all these prime positions are becoming vacant."

"Why bother with retail stores if you are doing so well without them? Why take on all the costs of leases, staff and management…?"

"Well the original reason we opened stores was to help bankrupt MFI. We started opening up alongside MFI stores because while they were spending twenty-five thousand pounds a week on advertising, all I had to do was set up next-door and open. Being so close to them I needed no advertising whatever. All I had to do was sit there and sponge off their advertising. So they spent the twenty-five grand and it was like I'd spent twelve and a half grand but I hadn't. So I was a leech."

I laughed and said, "Nothing wrong with being a leech. They're coming back into fashion. Now – going back to your sales system, as I understand it you have what you call designers who act as salesmen."

"Yeah. We receive inquiries and book appointments for

salesmen – designers – to go out and visit. They usually manage four appointments in a day. And we found a lot of business from Trade Shows both in England and around the world."

"But I thought you said you were banned from Trade Shows in Britain."

"Oh, God, yeah, yeah. We've been banned. But we don't go under our own name. We use a different name and let 'em know who it is halfway through the fair."

"So your main sales effort through your designers is simple, inexpensive and effective."

"Yeah. It keeps costs down and works well. We're just opening up in Ireland and planning to use the same system."

"Are you finding that a good market?"

"Well, we're right at the beginning in Ireland; training staff and looking for premises to open our own warehouse. We already sell there but we can't cope with the level of enquiries the way we're doing it now, by sending a full truckload of kitchens every week from here. This week's truck carried thirty-eight kitchens. We can sell around two hundred kitchens a week in Ireland when we're located there. So not only do I get a chance to go at the Irish market, I can also attack Britain by exporting from there. Under Irish laws, Trading Standards in Britain can't attack me when I'm not a British company."

"So how will you export from Ireland?"

"I'll bring goods from China to my new warehouse in Southern Ireland and deliver from there to my wholesale customers in Britain – other kitchen manufacturers – without any bullshit difficulties. And I don't have to follow British laws. For instance, I don't need a heavy truck operating licence. The bastards here in Oldham took away my operating licence but my trucks from Ireland won't need a British operating licence. I won't have to follow any British criteria so I'll have my Irish business delivering kitchens to England and Northern Ireland on my Irish registered trucks and it'll be 'Up Yours' with your fookin' criteria, pals. It'll be easier to ship direct from China to Ireland instead of to Maple Mill then shipping on and we'll have lots of advantages."

"Going back to the way you advertised – did you take on an advertising agency?"

"No. A long time ago I opened my own advertising agency as a registered company but only to get the fifteen per cent advertising fee. A few other companies tried the same so they changed the laws and to be recognised as an agency now you must have at least three clients, so I got mates that had businesses to become clients and we handle their advertising too."

"And which medium is the main thrust of your advertising now?"

"Newspapers are good for bringing in business?"

" Yeah. Internet inquiries are increasing all the time"

"How do Internet customers find you?"

"They just put the word kitchens in the computer and up we pop, right at the top."

"How long have you been on the Internet?"

"About eighteen months."

"Do you still use motorway advertising?"

"No."

"Some television or no television?"

"No television. We only do newspapers, magazines and Internet."

"And are enquiries through the Internet increasing?"

"Yes, definitely."

"So from a business point of view you're moving very much with the times. Did you take advice on Internet advertising or was it your idea?"

"Well, it's trial and error, isn't it? You try something and if it works you stick with it."

"But publicity can work both ways. The bad publicity against you as a businessman and against your companies over the past eight years would have killed any other business but you still thrive and, as far as I understand, you're still expanding, despite the current severe recession. Is that correct?"

"Yeah."

"So are you saying that eight years of legal actions against you personally and your business, along with enormous Trading Standards pressure and the terrible media coverage has not affected your business?"

"Of course it has. It's made life a lot harder, in terms of selling. Whereas we're successful now we would have been ridiculously successful if all this bullshit had not been thrown at us. So although it's made life hard, it's also made me more determined, I suppose."

"But despite all that you are saying that you've done better than most of your competitors?"

"Oh yeah – a damned sight better. But a lot of it is because I've never had time for bank managers and bullshit like that and sitting doing business plans and all the rest of it. I always felt that whatever money I want, I'd be faster to earn it rather than suck up to these idiots."

"So, apart from the one time when you had the loan from Barclays that was withdrawn, you've never borrowed money?"

Vance propped himself up again and in a raised voice began again to fight old battles.

"No. Apart from that I've never borrowed money," he almost

shouted. "And I've never bothered with selling shares and all the bullshit that goes with it. I call it Wine Bar Business – all this invisible money that exists. The sort of money that kept MFI and all these public limited companies afloat for so long. They're allowed to lose hundreds of millions each year yet carry on. I don't understand *how* you can carry on, losing millions. If I lost one million this year I'd be bankrupt. How do they *do* it? It's these clever people that grab money from bankers and the public…"

Seeing this tirade could continue a long time I broke in and asked, "So have you ever actually had an overdraft?"

"Well, I had the bank loan we spoke of a minute ago to help build the first factory in China."

"Yes, but that's a *loan* for a specific purpose. Have you ever had an operating overdraft?"

"No."

"Never?"

"No. Never."

"So you've done it all on your own money, and, of course, that saves you a lot of money in bank interest and I suppose you'd put big bank loans and borrowings down as a large factor in the death of companies like MFI?"

This question irritated Vance and he snapped, "I've told you why they went bust. Instead of only one man in charge they had management running the company. Management only care about how long its salary will go on for. If the company goes bust in six months time it doesn't matter – they've had six months salary and can look for another job somewhere. They don't lose anything, only a job, and anyone can get a bloody job if they have half a brain. They don't lose their homes or anything like that, so they've no *real* reason for *wanting* to make it work."

"So you're saying that what you've done in making a very successful business is extremely simple – only use your own money out of business earnings?"

"Yeah."

"And you've used only your own money to develop the British business, with just the bank loan for a short time for the Chinese business. Do you see this as a major reason for your continuing survival while others fail?"

"Yes. They're strapped up in debt, aren't they?"

"So what size do you think your business is in relation to the others now? You used to think you were fourth largest in Britain. What do you reckon now?"

"Well, now that number one, MFI, have gone, we're probably number three, with Magnet now number one and B&Q number two."

"What about Moben?"

Vance snorted in derision. "Moben? They're fookin' nothing – they're poxy. And they managed to lose twenty million last year."

"Do you supply these people with parts from China without them knowing?"

"We supply them through others, yeah."

"And they don't know the product is coming from you?"

"No, not really."

"And what do you supply them?"

"Doors, handles, glass, and other things from China. We don't supply direct to them. We supply to their suppliers in England – big people who manufacture for them and take full container loads. And we supply raw materials like PVC that goes on kitchen tops. We get that from Korea."

"And do these people supplying your competitors know they are buying from you?"

"Those people buying off me and selling on – they know – but they just keep quiet."

"To change the subject – what has been the effect on you personally of all the eight years of pressure?"

The question seems to puzzle him. He frowned, paused for several seconds; clicked his tongue again and said. "Pressure... Pressure? What do you mean?"

"Well... All the physical and mental pressure you must have

been under for all that time. Pressure on you personally."

Still apparently confused by the question he drops into a long pause that shows as almost twenty five seconds on my digital recorder. For the first time since I met him, he seems completely stumped, lying back on the pillows, teeth clicking against tongue and staring at the ceiling as though trying to understand the question.

To break the moment I say, "You must have been very strong."

This jerks him back to action. He sits up and says, "Oh yeah. If I didn't keep fit and go training and things like that I wouldn't have been able to survive."

"But you need to be mentally strong as well."

"Yeah. Course you do."

He stops and frowns again as though never confronted by such an idea, before saying, "Well, they picked on the wrong guy didn't they? If they'd picked on a normal guy he'd have crumbled. Everything they've done is designed to make the normal guy crumble." He chuckles. "Well, I wasn't fookin' normal to begin with and you can't really send an already mad man mad, can you?"

"When you say you are not normal, what do you mean?"

"Well. Since being a teenager I've been in jail many times in many different countries, I've been shot and been in circumstances that a normal guy would never, never get himself into. And as I've said before the first week in jail's the hardest, the second week's the second hardest but after the third week it gets easier and easier until it's no longer a deterrent, it's just an inconvenience. That's how it gets you. So now, if you threaten me with prison and things like that I just say "Oh, get on with it if that's what you want," I just consider it part of the job."

"In other words, circumstances strengthened you mentally and you kept yourself strong physically?"

"Yeah. Exactly. I've been hardened up from the beginning and if you throw something at me I just compare it to the worst thing that's happened in the past and think, oh well, I got over that so I'll be able to get over this."

After a short silence while Vance seems to run through his past problems with bowed head and half-closed eyes, I return him to the present by asking, "Here we are in 2009 with a very deep recession and companies going bust everywhere. Now what effect…"

Jolting back to life again, Vance anticipates my question. "I've been waiting for this moment. This is my opportunity," he snaps.

"Tell me," I say.

"This recession was due five years ago. I just couldn't understand why it didn't happen. And every year – every day since then – I've been saying to people 'We're going to have the biggest fookin' recession you've ever seen in your life.' It's overdue. The bubble popped five years ago but somebody patched it up and we've carried on blowing the thing up. It's false; it's bullshit, it's invisible. We've put the price of property up to generate more money for the country; we're totally overvalued on the overseas market and caused our own downturn in manufacturing."

"You think that?"

"Let me answer your question. I've been waiting for this recession to happen and rubbing my hands and waiting and wondering why isn't it happening yet and now it has happened it's big opportunities time for me isn't it, with all those guys who dealt in invisible money gone?"

"But how is it an opportunity for your companies *specifically?*"

"Because last year if you had a house worth three hundred grand and you only had a hundred grand in it, you had two hundred grand the bank was willing to lend you. So if the husband wanted a BMW he'd walk straight into the BMW garage and buy one. If the wife wanted a new kitchen she'd walk into Magnet and they'd say, 'It's fifteen grand,' and she'd say, 'Yes I'll have that,' with no thought of, 'Why should I save money? It's only fifteen grand, the bank's just given me a hundred, two hundred…'"

I break in – "Yes but that's all theory. How *specifically* is the recession an opportunity for you?"

"I'm halfway through telling you."

"Sorry. Go on."

"Now all of a sudden that lady can't get that money from the bank so she can't just accept the first price offered; she's got to shop around now she's spending her own money instead of the bank's. She's got to be more prudent as to how this money's spent and where it's coming from. So now when she shops around and finds us she sees she can't find anyone cheaper. So the more she looks in magazines or the Internet, the more chance she has of finding us."

I jump into the rush of words to say, "But hang on a minute. Are you talking just about cheaper, or cheaper with high quality?"

"Yes. With high quality – our product is the best quality kitchen on the flat pack market. There's nothing to compare with it. So the recession's been good for me. More people are finding us because they're looking around more before buying. Controlling staff is easier because they can't just go off to another job down the road. Finding educated staff is easier. Showrooms are easier to move into 'cos there are so many empty. This time of recession is the time to go round building your business. It's no good building your business when things are on a high. Before, if you buy a hundred stores at a million pounds each and in a year's time they're only a hundred grand each, you've lost ninety percent of your investment. But now, in recession, if you're buying at a hundred grand each and in a few years they go back to a million, you're making nine *hundred* percent on your investment."

I break in to say, "Yes, but, to the outsider it would seem that houses are not being built and I know you have a trade section that sells to builders. So how is that doing?"

"The pond is smaller right now but we're becoming a much bigger fish in that pond."

"But with this smaller pond, if you sold, say twenty thousand kitchens a year up until 2008, have your actual sales increased or decreased during the recession?"

"We've maintained about the same rate of sale but our expenses have come down a lot. We're now a lot more wary – a lot more educated – we've got much cheaper advertising and got rid of poor staff and kept the good staff. More staff means more problems with more people to pass the buck to and fewer people to talk to. You get rid of the wonderful habit of passing things around. Too many people spend all day passing jobs around to each other and eventually nobody does those jobs. If instead of ten people you have two people doing a job they do it far better because they're responsible for it being done properly."

I ask, "Does the current maintaining of sales at previous levels include Ireland?

"Yeah. By moving into a new market we've brought back what we've lost in England. We do that all the time with different markets, so where we may be losing on one we are gaining in another, newer area. To stand still you have to go forward. If your aim is to stand still, you're actually going backwards."

"So you're saying that to keep going forward, you've moved from old-fashioned advertising to modern Internet advertising and seeing downturn in your traditional market you've moved to new markets to hold up your British business. So do you see yourself as well-placed for when an overall business upturn comes?"

"Yeah. I see the next ten years as getting everything together so I can sell out at the height of the next bubble."

"You mean sell the business?"

"Yeah."

"And do you consider that in the next ten years you might become the Number One kitchens supplier in Britain?"

Vance nods. "Yeah. No problem."

"You said that with great confidence."

"Yeah. I did."

We laugh together and I say, "Here's a different question. Has the current world trading situation affected your exports from

China?"

"Yes. America's down."

"Down or dead?"

"Down. Not dead. And Europe's down except for Eastern Europe, which is up."

"Is that not strange? Because from what I read in the papers Eastern Europe is in a poor general economic position."

"No, it's developing and catching up. It's like water levelling out. Where, before, a house in England cost three hundred thousand pounds and a house in Bulgaria cost ten thousand pounds, now they're levelling out. We're finding there is more money in the East so we're selling kitchens there as people are starting to improve their houses."

"And has any collapse of the internal Chinese economy affected your business in China?"

"No. China is showing me exactly the same opportunities as in England and I'm planning to go round renegotiating prices with suppliers. All the factories we buy from have machinery and production capacity they must keep going to remain profitable. So we can go in now and say, 'No, we're not going to give you a hundred pounds any more, we're going to give you sixty.'"

"And are you carrying on with your retail outlets in China?"

"Yes. Six months ago I decided to come out of it but then

the price of the pound devalued so much that every ten pence I earned in China became eighteen pence. So I thought, oh shit, a retail stores business may not be as good as I thought it would in China but now the Chinese Yuan is worth sixty or seventy percent more than it was then."

"How many stores are you now operating?"

"We had sixty-three a year ago but we closed twenty-three rubbish stores leaving forty that are still selling well. So we're now at a standstill in opening new stores and I'll just let it settle for a while. But what is strange is that the last time I saw you I said I was definitely going to close the whole retail down in China. But the currency change made a big difference. I had to think, 'Oh now there's a reason to keep some of the bastard stores open.'"

I laugh and say, "I remember you saying, 'I'll close the lot down in two months.'"

Vance laughs too and says, "Yeah but I have another big advantage since the China bubble burst. Nobody wants to go and invest in there any more. Before there was a fifty or sixty percent advantage to manufacturing in China but now it's down to only about twenty percent and that's not enough bait to encourage people, so the flow of new factory openings has stopped right across the country. When I started it cost about a million pounds to build and open a new factory. Now it costs four million pounds and that puts people off."

"So you are taking advantage of a changing world."

"Yeah. You're right. It's a changing world. What's bad today is good tomorrow and what's good today is bad tomorrow. Yeah."

## Chapter Eleven
# *Media Storm – The Blizzard Of Hate*

The Mill is a massive Victorian pile, cold and forbidding both inside and out. I sit swaddled by my overcoat in the ancient spinning hall now used as a large open plan office, riffling through a six-inch high pile of newspaper pages. Culled from local and national press and sorted into precise date order they show a fascinating story of the press whipping several small local news items into a national media storm.

Within a few minutes I forget the chill air and the bustle of business going on around me and become caught up in a chase that starts slowly then builds over six years to a crescendo

The early local press stories, written before Vance's move to The Mill, are bland, informative and quite accurate. The Manchester Evening News (MEN) refers to the business operating from Vance's gym and the move to larger premises in Bury New Road. This is the time when Vance admits to selling "crap" kitchens and the phrase "Kitchen Rogue" appears as an easy media title for Vance.

Around 2001 a few stories appearing in local Manchester and Oldham papers investigate complaints from dissatisfied customers about Vance's rickety kitchens business and Oldham Trading Standards (OTS) begin to increase pressure on Vance.

"At that time they were right," he says. His kitchens, rejects or salvage from other companies' manufacturing errors, were poorly finished in Vance's workshop or delivered missing vital parts. His place in those days at the outer boundaries of Britain's kitchen industry relied on the hope that customers accepted poor quality in exchange for ridiculously low prices.

Newspaper stories and OTS press releases concentrated on the number of complaints received at the OTS office. Only muted mention of Vance's criminal past come through in hints that this dodgy businessman is at it again, so no accusations or taunts of direct criminality yet appear.

What started as a gentle breeze of local press innuendo and inaccurate complaints figures developed into a brisk wind when some national newspapers picked up Manchester reports of legal moves to stop Vance trading using the new Stop Now Order. This complex law, apparently originating in the EU, aims to disrupt dishonest traders by using Contempt of Court rules if a business they control makes any mistake, however minor, in the manufacture or delivery of goods.

Vance tells me, "I can break that law just by getting out of bed in the morning if any of the silly buggers working for me send out one wrong hinge in a three-thousand part kitchen."

He overcame this by resigning ownership of his kitchens business and passing day to day management to others – people trusted from school or years of friendship – keeping only an advisory role as far as the outside world is concerned.

But the outside world picked up first use of this strange new law, when in May 2002 The Sunday Times printed an article about Vance and the Stop Now Order. The piece stated that Vance's business was subject to 180 complaints a year, showing that the journalist had, at least, bothered to check facts. This article is almost the last to show figures anywhere near correct but seemed to set the tabloids off on a six-year media storm that came across in the pile of newsprint before me as a howling blizzard of hate. Based on biased, fantastical and in the main, completely inaccurate complaints figures, the stories seem never to delve for fact nor check the drivel they shove out with such arrogant glee.

Sitting in that cold office, squinting at six years worth of smudged newsprint, I see how these stories, when read separately over a period of widely separated dates, would appear authoritative to the casual reader in their logical path of disclosure. But reading through several hundred pages all at the same time, obvious cracks and similarities appear in stories so settled and similar they run in a line from tabloid to tabloid and back again.

Choose any scurrilous Red Top and read about Vance then read again a few months later in other Red Tops and you see the same article repeated almost word for word. Same attack, same unflattering photograph, same triumph at Red Top investigative ability. Only the newspaper name and journalist byline differ. It seems so simple. Just type the name "Vance Miller" and bring up a computer template story already laid out and easily cribbed with only the date and a few hints at journalistic cleverness changed.

Article after article over the six years add drama by "revealing" Vance to the world, or "at last stopping this rogue from his dodgy trading." None seemed to notice that having "revealed" or "stopped" Vance last year or the year before they are repeating the same nonsense from their own rags and from their competitors.

And in all the naming and shaming and "stopping this rogue/ conman /gangster" from trading, none appear to notice that Vance is far from "stopped" or bankrupt or skulking in some overseas hideaway with ill-gotten loot. Nope! He continues developing his business with remarkable success both in Britain and China, whilst watching his household-name competitors go bust.

Up until November 2006 all the media and Trading Standards pressure on Vance and his business is based on stressing and reporting customer complaints with only vague unsubstantiated hints at criminal behaviour by use of the word "conman" or "conned".

The real media hunt-and-chase-let's-get-this-man probably started with a Manchester Evening News article in April 2002 stating that seventy five percent of Vance's customers complained about kitchens worth around three million pounds. This seems based on an OTS press release in December 2001 at the start of the Stop Now case, commenting on "a very large number of complaints," with no hint of how many.

This allowed some newspapers to set out hilariously silly and contradictory figures without ever appearing to check and research a source. The Daily Express in January 2004 gives a figure of 180 complaints in a year. Pretty close. The actual figure for that year in Oldham Trading Standards records is 185. The People in August 2004 gives the same figure of 180. Following stories throughout the press become wilder and more reckless, grabbing any figure that came to mind in the heat of the moment.

On 29th November 2006, one hundred and thirty Police and Trading Standards officers mounted an enormous and aggressive dawn raid on The Mill and Vance's home. Police handcuffed and arrested Vance and dragged him to Oldham Police cells for a day and night of questioning. At The Mill officials took every scrap of paper from the offices, including family holiday pictures from the walls, and every vestige of computer equipment and records and emptied Vance's house of all document, telephones and other equipment.

On 30th November the Daily Mirror reported The Mill Raid in breathless excitement, shouting, "50,000 complaints and millions of pounds conned in five years of trading." The figure '50,000' could be read as the number of complaints in one year or it makes a neatly rounded calculation for tabloid readers of 10,000 complaints per year over the five years.

Simple to understand but nowhere near correct. The official 2006 Oldham Trading Standards record shows 73 complaints for that year, which makes the headline 9,927 out.

On the same day The Express, The Star, The Mail seemed happy to report by implication 50,000 complaints per year without bothering to ask how a business selling 400 kitchens a week (The Mail, 30th November 2006) manages to garner complaints almost sixty per cent higher than the number of kitchens sold?

Especially since an Office Of Fair Trading press release dated 9th January 2007 showed all complaints against all kitchen companies in Britain to be 12,819 during the whole of 2006, the same year Vance took 73 complaints.

If I found that out all on my own, why couldn't these large

newspapers so richly endowed with staff and researchers try the same path of analysis, curiosity and research?

Even the famously august and campaigning publication WHICH! Magazine failed on this score by, in January 2007, publishing the same old chestnuts from the previous five years.

The WHICH! article commenting on the Mill Raid, spouts that "15,000 people are thought to be have been conned out of millions" and "Trading standards officers said they handle between 60 and 100 complaints a week about the firm, making it the UK's most complained about company." This equals 3000 to 5000 complaints in a year, quite a long way from the official 2006 Oldham Trading Standards listing of 73.

So on 24th December 2007 I sent an Email to Susanne at WHICH! explaining the contradiction of news media quoting entirely wrong complaints figures – anything from 180 per year (Sunday Times) to 50,000 (People) to any figure in between as apparently plucked from the air by the journalist. Mentioning the latest shot of 3000 complaints per year in Oldham Evening Chronicle, I pointed out that the true annual figure of 73 complaints equals 1.5 per week, not the completely false 60 to 100 in the WHICH! article.

"Any retraction and correction?" I asked.

No reply, so a month later I called and spoke with Sarah Gartside in the WHICH! public relations department and followed with an Email giving the correct information. Accepting they may have published incorrect figures in good faith I suggested that, now possessing the truth, why not print a correction?

No reply so I sent the Email again to Sarah, repeating my suggestion for a retraction and suggested a meeting to discuss the figures. In reply I received some well written waffle about maintaining the highest standards of accuracy, blah-blah and that the figures were taken from an OTS press release in November 2006.

Ah yes. That Oldham Trading Standards press release, used as a get-out by several newspapers. A wondrous document sending out completely inaccurate figures absolutely ignoring the correct figures their office releases to the likes of me who have the gumption to ask and check.

My contact with WHICH! ended by me pointing out that the magazine is definitely at fault in not investigating that information supplied is correct. I wrote, "In this case you showed gullibility in trusting an inaccurate figure without making simple checks. I doubt your editor will feel the need to make any adjustment to the faulty information. As I am dealing in verifiable facts I will place our exchange of correspondence on this matter in my book."

Oh dear. I received a sharp final bit of blah from Sarah that included, "We reject your claim that our printing of the figures in January 2007 was "wrong and inaccurate" and we would point out that we are entitled to rely on figures from Trading Standards without the need for further verification."

Oh really? What then is the point of being an investigative magazine?

Ms Gartside also felt, "We do not think that there is anything further to add to this issue." Well, I suppose not when you've been caught out, as a Red Top might say.

So where do all these fictional figures come from?

I called other publications and asked the question. All told me "From Oldham Trading Standards." Odd. Because the actual complaints against Vance and his business between 2001 and 2006, the year of The Mill Raid, total 785 complaints over five years – an average of 130 per year. The figure jumps in 2007 because of The Raid and problems associated with all paperwork being confiscated. A full set of figures and analysis appears in Appendix 1.

During the middle period of this storm of hate, television began to take interest in Vance. In succession he appeared in *Rogue Trader, The UK's Worst* and *Watchdog*. All retailed the same inaccuracies to make absolutely certain that Vance came across as a dishonest rogue. Around this time someone coined the description "Kitchen Gangster". I fail to discover whether the title came from tabloid, television or Vance himself, as he does tend to overact and send himself up for the media. But it stuck, for again and again it is used as an easy headline.

The Oxford English Dictionary defines Fraud as "**1.** Wrongful or criminal deception intended to result in financial or personal gain. **2.** A person intending or thing intended to deceive."

Note the word "Intending." The tirade of abuse against Vance appears mostly brought about not through deliberate, planned fraud but by customer complaints of quite minor delivery faults or errors or misunderstanding by either the customer or Vance's office. Most errors were quickly corrected to satisfy most of the aggrieved customers, except one or two who appear to have enjoyed Red Top attention.

The media take no account that the tiny average annual incidence of consumer complaints against Vance calculates to a smidgeon over two percent of the 20,000 kitchens his company delivers per year.

This barrage of hate seems egged on by Oldham Trading Standards whom everyone blames for passing the amazingly inaccurate figures squirted around by the tabloid press. Hardly any publication uses a basis of fact to show a true picture.

When I ask reporters, "Why?" most shrug and say, "Don't know." Although a couple of newsmen intimate some possible undercover intrigue by the Oldham authorities using Trading Standards as their instrument of attack.

On 9th January 2007 in a Press Release faxed out by Marc Dubin of Oldham Trading Standards, Tony Allen, head of OTS, issued a statement advising consumers against "…dealing with Mr Miller or the company, which operates under the name Kitchens." In the Release Mr Allen states, "There is a high probability of consumer detriment, misrepresentation, fraud and problems with this firm."

This Release and statement appeared in a newspaper called Guernsey Press. Naturally, anyone reading this piece in Guernsey would assume Vance is a convicted fraudster. I can find no other newspaper using such language, since at no time to date has Vance ever been convicted of fraud. So is it possible other newspapers feel the need to be careful of the precise words they publish, when, perhaps, a Press Release is suspect?

It is true that following the Big Mill Raid Vance has been *charged* with fraud but at time of writing these charges have yet to be tested in court. So how can such a statement be made without challenge?

Oldham Trading Standards, who themselves appear to have

difficulty in offering the press accurate complaints figures from their own records, seem to the independent observer equally loose with the language of this Press Release. The wording and attitude behind it could strike our independent observer as a form of oppression and a "public relations exercise" calculated – in the words of the judge criticising Trading Standards in another case – to be designed to attract "sensationalist" publicity

The Daily Telegraph business section of 15th February 2008 reports a case dealing with an investigation into milk price-fixing in 2002 by large supermarkets in detail. The article says, "In a strongly worded press release (in September 2007) the OFT claimed that collusion had cost consumers £270 million," and quoted the OFT Release as stating, "This is a very serious case. We believe supermarkets have been colluding to put up the price of dairy products."

Those mentioned in the article include Asda, Tesco and Morrison's. All denied any wrongdoing and Morrison's went to court asking for a judicial review in the way the OFT publicised its "controversial and high profile" investigation. Morrison's followed up the judge's agreement to the judicial review with a separate libel action centred on the Press Release.

Our independent observer may feel that this case shows very similar pressure and publicity placed upon Vance by Oldham

Trading Standards and other authorities. Supermarkets with deep pockets and top lawyers can fight back. I asked Vance why he did not do the same. His reply. "Let the bastards do their best. There's no doubt Tony Allen has got it in for me but he and Oldham Council haven't managed to close me down yet in six years of trying. Let the bastards keep wasting their money by chasing me. I don't give a shit."

After five or six hours sifting through this pile of newsprint, I find myself wondering how to excavate some truth from this mountain of misinformation? I wonder if a meeting with the man Vance sees as his nemesis and main enemy, Tony Allen, head of Oldham Trading Standards might help.

# Chapter Twelve
## *Lion's Den*

On a cold February morning I stumble up icy steps and into the squat 1950s style building that holds Oldham Trading Standards offices.

My welcome from Tony Allen is pleasant and I am offered tea. He is younger than I expected – his exalted position and high Trading Standards profile suggests someone older.

When first I requested a meeting, the OTS lawyer wanted a list of questions.

I replied, "How can I give a list of questions for a complex interview? I start with a subject and the conversation wanders from there and could go anywhere. I am not a journalist, I'm not looking for sensation, I'm not looking for headlines; I'm an author seeking fact about the OTS attitude to Vance Miller and his business."

"Yes but what is the point of the meeting?"

"In this project I am completely neutral. I offer no support for either side and express no opinions. I have full and open access to

Vance Miller, his factory, his staff, and any documents I request. Any question I ask is answered fully and openly. The actual words spoken appear in the book without editing. If I can't talk to Oldham Trading Standards and to Tony Allen in particular, my book will be awfully one-sided. Is that what you want?"

No one connected with Vance thought I had a chance of getting such an interview and expressed great surprise at my success. But here I am, sipping tea and being introduced to Jenny Barker, Media Communications Officer and Simon Bithel, a solicitor with the council.

Tony Allen starts our meeting by describing himself as head of Trading Standards and Licensing in Oldham and with no objection to my digital recorder commences a detailed explanation of his function in Trading Standards.

He says, "You are obviously aware that the Council is in the process of prosecuting Mr Miller so we have a number of restrictions that we're under because of the charges against him and the restrictions are imposed upon us by law. There are some things I might like to go into in more detail but can't."

I say, "I fully understand and from my point of view if you say something in error or as a slip of the tongue, please tell me and it will be struck out and not used."

Tony Allen says, "In your research you will have found there is a wide range of things that have been said about this case in the media or around. Some of it is stuff we have said and some of it is stuff we've been alleged to have said but haven't said and some stuff which is… we don't know where it's come from, so we'll be able to clarify some of that for you."

I say, "I fully understand. I have seen good and bad written about Miller and good and bad written about you, much of it obvious nonsense. I mean, you've probably seen yourself on the Internet and for the need of accuracy in the book I need fact, not opinion – not anybody's opinion – so I have to see as many people as I can. I have a list of questions that we may use as an agenda and any question you don't like, I will perfectly understand."

Tony Allen nods assent.

I continue, "I've broken the list into a sequence – Complaints, Newspapers and from Miller's point of view, Harassment. I stress specifically that the Harassment section is from *his* point of view and not my opinion. I have no opinion."

Tony Allen interrupts and continues his explanation of the function and practice of Trading Standards.

Finally the interview starts with my first question, "When did Miller first come to the notice of Trading Standards?"

"In Oldham, in 2001 when he moved to The Mill. Prior to that he was under the attention of Rochdale where he had another mill."

"So Trading Standards were on to him before he moved to Maple Mill in Oldham."

"Yes."

"Was his…perceived method of operation passed on to you by Rochdale or did you pick it up yourselves?"

"The bulk of what we were aware of at first relates to a case against him and Craftsman Kitchens in April 2002 by Rochdale. The answer to your question is that we probably got most of our knowledge in the way Miller operates from our colleagues in Rochdale. But he didn't come under our direct attention until he moved to Oldham in 2001."

I say, "A major part of the pressure on Miller and his business is this question of complaints. Oldham Trading Standards have been reported as saying that Miller received fifty thousand complaints per year."

"We've never said that."

"I know, but your own documents state that Miller receives sixty to one hundred complaints a week."

"We don't… let me put it in context. In the run up to the Mill Raid we were dealing with sixty to one hundred complaints a week. We have said that. What we have never given is a complete figure of the numbers of complaints, principally because we don't know the complete figure. And we've never given an indication to the extent of how the figures have accelerated or decelerated."

I break in to say, "I have figures that I'll show you…"

Tony Allen interrupts me to say, "We'll come back to that. We then amended what we said to say that we continue to receive a substantial number of complaints without the number."

"So if I ask you what you consider a substantial number, what would you…"

Interrupting again, he says, "We wouldn't comment on that. We simply say at the moment that we continue to receive a substantial number, using words like, 'more than you would normally accept.,"

I say, "It is interesting to me that only one newspaper appears to have anything correct and that is The Times where they report one hundred and eighty complaints in a year. All other newspapers quote your sixty-to-one-hundred a week, calculating to over five thousand a year. Like you I have to work on averages and what I have here…"

Tony Allen interrupts again to explain about reorganisation of the way Trading Standards now collect statistics centrally. I try to break in to say I have those central statistics but he talks over me and continues explaining in detail how Trading Standards now collects and collates complaints against traders centrally to avoid double counting. He finishes by saying; "There has been a transition period between 2002 and 2007 when figures have not been particularly accurate."

I say, "Yes but they are obviously the only figures we have to work on. I went to the Office Of Fair Trading in London and obtained figures about Miller and his company from July 2004 to end December 2007. The figures I have from your office are from April 2004 to end November 2007. If I pass you these pages showing you my analysis of the figures for the two time periods you will see that the national OFT figures give twenty-one complaints a week throughout Britain and the figures from here – from this Oldham office – show eighteen complaints a week. This gives rise to several questions, such as, why are there so many complaints from here, from this office?"

Tony Allen shakes his head. "No. I'd say that isn't correct. Actually by far the majority of complaints are outside the Oldham area. In reality we rarely get complaints from Oldham residents."

I continue, "I analysed complaints through Oldham Trading Standards and the pressure on Miller is based on these figures. It is fairly obvious from the OTS figures that the year before the Mill Raid there were only seventy-three complaints, which equals one a week, but the year after the Raid complaints shot up to one thousand eight hundred and fifty three. I imagine there are two reasons for that; one being the extreme amount of ridiculous press coverage of which you know, and something issued from your office that appeared on Amazon that refers to three thousand complaints in a year.

"For the twelve months following the Raid, complaints figures drop as the pressure goes off. Now through all this pressure from newspapers and television, the business has not in any way slowed down. The outside observer looking at this will see that if Miller is selling twenty thousand kitchens a year and you receive approximately a hundred complaints, then Miller has nineteen thousand nine hundred satisfied customers, a point never spoken of by you or the press. And the top ten national complaints figures list of companies complained against throughout Britain shows complaints against fitted kitchens companies last year as twelve thousand eight hundred and nineteen and against large domestic appliances, thirty thousand, four hundred and twenty five.[1]

"So if you take that as about forty two thousand officially recorded complaints involving kitchens, the number of complaints being shown in the newspapers as complaints against Miller and his companies, totals every kitchen complaint in Britain plus ten thousand. It strikes me as very unfair that every complaint in

---

1        See Appendix 2

Britain plus ten thousand is being blamed on Miller."

Tony Allen breaks in and says, "Now just stop a second there, John. We haven't in any way published any of these figures to any of the media."

"You've published sixty to one hundred a week."

"Yes. That was in the weeks running up to the Raid."

"That brings us to another question. I am not being argumentative with you in any way. I am speaking of research I've done and facts unearthed that show you put the sixty-to-a-hundred a week statement out in July 2007 that totals over five thousand…"

Tony Allen interrupts to say, "I don't accept it totals five thousand because it is sixty to a hundred a week. You are making assumptions."

I interrupt back, "The figures are put out by Trading Standards over your name and the timing is not relevant to what I am trying to say. Although your weekly figure appeared in July 2007 the newspapers are still picking up exactly the same tired old figure and tired old story and rehashing old stories without further enquiry or checks. An interesting question to an outsider like me to ask is, if those figures are being attributed to you and we all know they are wrong, have you…"

Tony Allen interrupts again to say," Sorry. I don't accept they are wrong."

"But figures from your own department's show they are wrong."

"Your extrapolation of figures might be wrong but I don't accept our figures are wrong."

"But they are. For instance, figures from April to November 2007 show five hundred and sixty six complaints. Now, that is eleven a week, not sixty-to-a-hundred. Those figures are from you. I have your letter here."

I wave the letter and offer it to be read. "I am not being argumentative. I am speaking of facts and there they are. The question I ask as an outsider is if the figure being given out is wrong and the newspapers are still putting pressure on Miller at the original figure with no change, why are the figures not being corrected? As I understand it the Trading Standards task is to help mediate and despite the fact Miller is going to court with around twenty-four charges, in the interest of fairness and factuality, someone should correct that wrong information. So is it going to be corrected?"

"That is not something I can discuss today."

"I don't know if you give Miller and his company details of complaints?

"Yes we do. And there is another aspect to this you may wish to consider in relation to your figures. The reason being there are at least twelve and we think possibly more companies in his name."

"Yes. I know about that and I have a list of companies from your department giving names, some incorrect."

We studied a letter from Kirsty Robins to advertisers asking for information about Miller and his companies, among them companies and people's names nothing to do with Miller. I suggest this is another inaccurate document from the Oldham Trading Standards office.

"This is something I cannot discuss," says Tony Allen, "As it is part of ongoing investigations."

"That is of no consequence to me but I have made my point that here is something published from your office that is inaccurate in referring to Miller."

"As I say, inaccurate or not it is part of the investigating process and is subject to the courts."

"That is fine but on another point, the Office Of Fair Trading on 27th August 2006 actually advertised for complaints about Miller's company. I am interested to know on what authority they are allowed to advertise for complaints against a company?"

"That is not a matter for us. That is a matter for the OFT."

"Ok. On a different subject, do you ever get any feedback on complaints resolved?"

"Yes."

"Satisfactorily resolved?"

"Yes. Of course it depends on the specific complaint and the company."

"And when you do get such a note, do you tell the companies or not?"

"It depends on the circumstances but we do keep contact with companies involved and close out the file."

I pause for a moment then ask, "Because one of the problems shown as a complaint I found during research related to one woman who had something wrong with a kitchen and went down to Maple Mill where the matter was solved to her satisfaction. She then went home and through OTS claimed £33.00 for travel expenses. Now that will appear in your figures as a complaint but seems to me to be terribly minor but about which you wrote a letter to Maple Mill. Why should such a minor matter be subject to a letter to the company and so becomes an official complaint? Is this not where, perhaps, Trading Standards should mediate?"

"I can't comment on an individual complaint."

"Ok. There is another question about the general pressure put on Miller. It relates to indications by Trading Standards that there may be fraud if customers deal with Miller. Now I don't believe that he has ever been convicted of fraud nor previously charged with fraud. Do you have any information on that?"

"I can't comment on that. But what I will say about the line we are taking…we have been and remain concerned at the significant number of complaints we continue to receive about this firm despite the Stop Now Order, despite the Advertising Standards rulings, despite charges that have been brought by Trading Standards and despite the advice and information we provide to the company on their management practices. It is our carefully considered view that it is not in the best interests of consumers to enter into arrangements with Vance Miller and his companies."

"But are you correct in saying that? Are you correct to use the phrase in your Press Release that I now read; 'There is a high probability of consumer detriment, misrepresentation, fraud and problems with transactions'. Is it correct to say such a thing since he has never been convicted of fraud – I know he has been charged but there has been no case yet –so why, in 2007, should the phrase be used?"

"It was carefully considered."

"I ask because I was very interested to read this article in the Daily Telegraph. Have you seen it?" I reached in and pulled out the paper, "Have you seen it?"

"No."

"The article is to do with accusations of milk price collusion by supermarkets."

Rustling the pages open I read out, "'Judge accuses OFT of 'PR hype' over inquiry.'

I stop and look up for reaction. None. So I say, " You can either photocopy it or I'll send you a copy but what the article says is, 'A High Court Judge slammed the OFT for engaging in public relations exercises and accused the regulator of trying to attract sensationalist publicity'."

I stop and look up again for reaction. None. So I continue reading, "...Mr Justice Davis's damning comments came as he granted supermarket Morrison's to seek a judicial review of the way the OFT publicised its controversial and high-profile investigation into the alleged price-fixing of milk. "The article continued to say that '...the OFT claimed in a Press Release that collusion on milk prices had cost two hundred and seventy million pounds' and continued, 'This is a very serious case. We believe supermarkets have been colluding in putting up the price of dairy products...'"

I pause again. Still no reaction so I continue reading, "... Morrison's have since instigated libel proceedings, centred on the Press Release. In his ruling, Mr Justice Davis stated, 'The original Press Release seems to me to illustrate the dangers of bodies such as Office Of Fair Trading engaging in public relations exercises to attract potentially sensationalist publicity via the media.'"

Again I found no reaction from Tony Allen so read a little more of the Judge's comment about the OFT thereafter beating a retreat and adopting altogether more objective language both in correspondence and in subsequent purported clarification.

Still no reaction so I said, "When I read that the other day it rang a bell so I went back through other newspapers and I did find you actually quoted in a Guernsey newspaper using similar style of phrase."

At this point Tony Allen started to interrupt but I raised a finger and stopped him – "Let me finish the question." I showed him the Guernsey newspaper and asked, "Since there is absolutely no record anywhere of Miller being at that time charged with fraud is it correct to suggest he is acting fraudulently?"

"I have no comment at this stage."

"Ok. That's fine."

"But to point you in the right direction; the legal position based on a High Court case in the year 2000 that relates to the Crown versus Liverpool City Council. In that case the court went through exactly what Trading Standards officers could and could not say in relation to their activities. That case is the basis upon which we relate with the Media and is a very important part of our overall strategy of protecting and informing consumers, which is very important in empowering consumers to make informed decisions. So our work with the Media is an important part of that as it set out parameters and guidelines to which we adhere and at all times everything we have said and done and published has been in line with that case."

I nod and say, "But I think to the outsider and especially based on the comments from Mr Justice Davis, one would be surprised at an official office stating fraud when there is no evidence of fraud from that individual."

"I can't comment on that and I don't accept what you just said."

"Fine. Now, may I turn to the business of Trading Standards applying what may appear to the outsider to be unfair pressure on Miller during the court case of Peaty versus Kitchens? The plaintiff complained that he ordered a real wood kitchen and instead received a kitchen made of chipboard. I have here the complete court transcript of the case, from which I'll read. It shows Peaty lost because evidence conclusively proved that he got what he ordered. I see that at one point, when under pressure, Peaty says 'I am here with my case in this circumstance and there have been three television programmes on exactly the same problems I am having now from exactly the same company. Hundreds of

Vance Makes The News
*Photo: John Newton*

Vance & Paul in the Maple Mill Office
*Photo: Vance Miller*

To get around rules banning foreigners travelling throughout rural China, Vance fitted out this bus with luxury accommodation and painted Olympic logos across it. He says, "It's illegal but if we get stopped by the police we just tell 'em we're the Olympic inspection committee here to check your grounds and whatnot."
*Photo: Vance Miller*

"Once I realised the prospects in China I was away a lot for anything between six weeks and six months but mostly, for seven or eight weeks at a time."
*Photo: Vance Miller*

Rather than depend on hundreds of suppliers spread across China, Vance aquired his own land and built his own factories to produce kitchen supplies.
*Photos: Vance Miller*

"I went round the villages and bought gold mining rights for three areas. So I had three shops, three gold mines, an export licence and spent my time rushing around the shops, and the gold mines, often getting down into the mine and digging with my Africans."

*Photos: Vance Miller*

"I talked to people in local government with authority to sell me a chunk of land. That's all a quarry is, just a big chunk of land, that's three or four acres in area but goes twenty acres down."

*Photos: Vance Miller*

"I needed to decide what's coming in to my factory. I needed to get involved with my own forest. Six thousand acres and we replant absolutely everything."
*Photos: Vance Miller*

"At the same time as buying land, buying a quarry, I was building two factories in China."
*Photos: Vance Miller*

The fire that destroyed much of Maple Mill.

# Fight your own blaze, boss told

A BUSINESSMAN has been ordered to personally put out a huge fire which destroyed his premises – or pay a £20,000 fine.

Vance Miller, 43, was left "completely devastated" after an inferno gutted his historic former cotton mill.

Amazingly fire crews were instructed to stop tackling the blaze while smoke was still billowing from the rubble.

Mr Miller was served a legal notice by his local council following complaints by residents of choking smoke drifting into their homes.

The order states it is Mr Miller's responsibility to tackle the blaze, which happened last month, in areas "inaccessible to the fire service".

He has now spent more than £20,000 buying specialist equipment and must work as a fire fighter from 8am to 8pm each day at the kitchen factory in Oldham, Greater Manchester.

Yesterday he told the Daily Express: "The mill is gutted along with £4million of machinery. I've got 250 employees and a business to run in the middle of a recession and I'm con-

## By David Pilditch

fined to fight a fire for 12 hours a day or face legal action. It's ridiculous.

"The letter says the fire is so immense and deep-rooted that they can't get to it, so go and get your own hosepipes, go and secure your own water supply and put it out yourself.

"I've had to scramble around parts of rubble that could collapse at any second and take me with it.

"There's no way on earth I am going to put any members of my staff at risk so I have got no option but to do the job myself."

Tony Ciaramella, assistant county fire officer at Greater Manchester Fire and Rescue Service, said a "lack of co-operation" with site operators had "resulted in the fire burning longer than necessary".

John Eley, assistant executive director at Oldham Council, said: "We are working with the mill owner, residents and partner organisations to ensure that these issues are resolved as quickly as possible."

News Article from the Oldham Evening Chronicle

Vance Fire Fighting
*Photo: Vance Miller*

people – two hundred people a week cannot possibly be wrong.'"

I pause for reaction. None, so I continue, "Then in reaction to denial of such a figure from the defendant, Peaty says, 'If you would care to make a single telephone call to Daniel Moore of Oldham Trading Standards, he will give you a complete insight into exactly how many complaints he is dealing with through Oldham Trading Standards in this company.'"

The judge: 'Tell me how many.

Peaty: 'Two hundred odd a day.

The defendant: 'I don't think so.

Peaty: 'Throughout the country.'"

I pause again before saying, "Now one can see that the figure Mr Peaty quotes is completely inaccurate based on the figures I have presented today from your own records. How can it be that a Trading Standards officer can – inverted commas – coach a witness in that way?"

I look at Tony Allen and say, "You're shaking your head."

"No. I'm just saying I don't know … you're quoting from this case… I don't know…"

"I'll let you have the transcript to copy."

Tony Allen shakes his head and mumbles "At this stage we're not prepared to… an officer was not a witness in that case."

"No he wasn't a witness but he obviously discussed the case in detail with the complainant."

After a frown and a pause Tony Allen says, "Oh… I don't know if that is the case or not but… we haven't… we have provided witness statements to County Courts. I don't know if we have in this case or not but it's irrelevant to the case we are on now…"

"But I'm not talking about the case you are on now. I'm talking about the pressure that is put onto the company or companies and, as far as reading this, the complainant was – inverted commas – *coached* to say something by Mr Moore of Oldham Trading Standards."

"I don't accept that and I haven't said it. I don't accept that in any way our officers coach witnesses."

"But I am saying it seems so to the *outsider,* you see…"

"You made a direct allegation there and…"

"I haven't made a direct allegation. I said *'to the outsider',* in inverted commas that the witness appears to have been coached."

"Well, let me be very clear, our officers do not coach witnesses."

"I am speaking directly of a court case in which this was said. I am making no allegations whatsoever."

"Ok… send me a copy of the case."

"I will. By all means."

A longish silence follows this minor spat whilst I shuffle papers and Tony Allen coughs a couple of times. Listening to the interview later, this seemed the only section where we move from polite exchange to nearly arguing.

I finish paper shuffling and switch with care to the Mill Raid by saying, "I know that current fraud charges against Miller relate to the Mill Raid so I will perfectly understand if you can't answer some questions about that Raid in, I think, October 2006."

He hastens to correct me, "November 29th, 2006."

"Ah yes. One of the problems Miller encountered after the Raid was that every single document in the building was taken; every computer and every single record of any kind – even, I am told – including photographs on the wall of children on holiday. And as a result of that he had problems in rebuilding the business. Hence, from Miller's point of view, this loss of information is one of the reasons complaints jumped in the following months, because his company had to rebuild their records by trying to find out who all their customers were. I stress, this is from the point of view of Miller and his staff. I am not making a statement of truth. So with this in mind, my question is… Why was all that documentation taken when your interest was historical? Because it gave the company enormous difficulty in trying to rebuild their knowledge base – which they have managed to do."

"That is very squarely part of the case."

"Ok. Fine. The other point is one you won't answer but – I am making a statement, based on your figures in June 2006, when the Mill Raid was being planned, according to your records the number of complaints in that period were seventy-three, which calculates to about one complaint a week. Since that figure is reasonably accurate, an outsider would be interested to know the basis of such an enormous Raid by one hundred and thirty officers?"

After a moment of silence Tony Allen says, "Before you move on let me say I don't accept that as a hypothesis. Let's move forward."

"So let us move to the matter of harassment. I am not saying that anyone is harassing Miller but looking at it from Miller's point of view; he appears to be being harassed. Now he, as you may know, is quite convinced that the reason for what he terms harassment comes down to proposed redevelopment of the Maple Mill area. I know there is a big plan – I've seen a copy of it – and I am interested if you have a comment about that. For instance, is there a plan to, say, knock down or completely redevelop The Mill in the way he thinks?"

"Personally I have no idea but I do know there are regeneration plans for that whole area. In terms of the use of the term 'harassment' I would say there is no way we are harassing Mr Miller or any of his associates. What we are engaged in is a concerted effort to deal with what is a substantial level of criminality. And we are using the powers that are at our disposal to do that in accordance with the law."

"I consider that a reasonable statement except I question the phrase 'criminality' because he has not yet been convicted of anything that Trading Standards have been putting to him. I know of some charges coming up but – you may like to confirm this – there are not yet any convictions for criminality based upon Miller's kitchens business. Am I correct?"

"They are in the process…"

I interrupt quite sharply to say, "I understand that but there is no *record* of Miller being *convicted* of criminality in this kitchens business. Am I correct?"

"In relation to this case, the case is coming before the courts… there are two cases…."

"Yes. But the question I then ask… is a body such as yourselves allowed – *before* a conviction – to use the phrase criminality?"

"Our role is as a criminal law enforcement agency. Our engagement is to look at trading criminality. That is what we are doing."

"In saying that are you *saying* that Miller is a criminal?"

"What I am saying is that we have investigated what, in our view, relates to criminality. If you listen carefully to what I am saying…"

"I am listening very carefully."

"If you take the example of a prolific burglar, the police will investigate a prolific burglar for being engaged in criminality. They will use the same process to prosecute him and put him before the courts. They will regard that behaviour as criminality. The burglar becomes a convicted criminal when the court convicts him and that is the same process we follow."

"I still query the use of the word 'criminality' before a man is convicted. But another point is that if complaints against Miller are – in truth – quite negligible taken in terms of the whole kitchens business in Britain…"

Tony Allen interrupts to say, "But, again, I don't accept that hypothesis."

"You may not think so but they are. If I may finish the point I'm making and then don't accept it. My point is that in the full year 2006 complaints against fitted kitchens companies throughout Britain totalled 12,819. That is the official Office Of Fair Trading figure. Miller's part in that – using your published complaints figures for the same period – calculate to just short of 1,410. National figures for large domestic appliances, which he also supplies and would, no doubt, be part of any of your complaints against him, total 304,245, giving a total of all such complaints as 317,000. This is why I use the word 'negligible' in using official figures to compare complaints against Miller and his kitchens business. Those figures are facts."

"No they are not."

"But they are the figures from the OFT."

"I don't accept those figures. Let me explain to you… Either the hypothesis of what you are saying about those complaints or the hypothesis in relation to the proportion of complaints against the national figures… What we will be doing is setting out exactly what those figures are when we come to the courts."

"Yes. But in my research I have to rely upon official figures from The Office Of Fair Trading. And those are the figures I am quoting to you. Here is a copy you can keep."

I hand over a copy and say, "As an outsider in all this I ask if you are you taking or proposing to take the same action against all the other kitchen companies who are party to at least as many, if not more, as Miller and his company?"

"I can't comment on that at all."

"We are now close to finishing. There were two incidents I find very odd and I have to ask if there was any involvement of Trading Standards. The first is that the bank that Miler used was given information to such an extent they closed Miller's bank account although he had plenty of money in there and had only a few months before received a letter from the bank on how well he ran his account. Was that a result of something from Trading Standards?"

"No, but I am aware of that but it wasn't anything that we instructed them to do or gave them information."

"So I doubt if you know who did it?"

"No I don't. But it is something they could perfectly legitimately have done off their own bat."

"I realise that but from private information I have heard, that is not the case."

"The other odd one is that when Miller flew to China, somebody told the airline that he is a security risk so the airline refused to bring him back. You may not know of this and may not be involved but naturally Miller thinks this is all part of the general harassment. Do you know anything of that?"

"No, that wouldn't have been us."

"Interesting isn't it? I wonder who that would have been."

"There are a number of potential candidates but it wouldn't have been us. That's not for me to speak of. It would not be part of our approach and certainly not sourced from us."

"Finally – this is almost a personal question, but it would be an outsider's question as well – I do know that the rules and regulations governing Trading Standards require mediation. I don't know, based on everything I've seen in my research that there is much thought on your part of mediating between Miller and complaining customers over the last number of years since you have been receiving these complaints. So why is there not more mediation?"

Simon Bithel the solicitor intervenes to almost whisper, "That is a question that inherently could affect the court case so I don't think…"

I laugh and say, "I don't agree but of course I accept you don't want to reply. I've finished so if you would care to ask me any questions I'll be happy to answer if I can."

"Just, really, what your plans are in timescale of publication. We are in the hands of the courts with the Quad Bike trial in March and…"

"So you are worried that anything I might write may impinge on the court?"

"No. What I'm concerned about is that we haven't been able to answer all of your questions, which we both knew would be the case, but I'm confident all your questions will be answered in the court during the trial which we anticipate will not be until next year."

"I would expect to publish after the case when a number of the unanswered questions will be resolved."

That ended the interview. I walked out into the chill Oldham air pleased with the welcome and Tony Allen's invitation after the recording finished to return for a further chat when the big court case we could not really mention is settled. "I'll hold you to that whatever the result," I said, shaking hands. As promised I transferred the interview to a CD and sent him a full copy but never received acknowledgement.

A few months later I saw Tony Allen in Manchester Crown Court at the Quad Bike Case. I am not sure he recognised me.

# Chapter Thirteen
## *The Big Mill Raid*

On 29th November 2006 at around five-thirty in the morning Police and Trading Standards officers staged a lightning raid on Maple Mill and Vance's house. At the same time they raided two other houses owned by managers from Vance's business. In total one hundred and thirty Police and Trading Standards officers took part in the raids.

This account of the Police action is very one-sided because Greater Manchester Police refuse to grant an interview to answer such questions as, why so many Police on what turned out to be a paper gathering exercise – a question ducked by Tony Allen in my interview with him. And who requested the raid? And who authorised such a massive operation on commercial premises? Based on the result – piles of paper, a few telephones and computers – it seems half a dozen officers could have done the same by knocking on the door with a simple warrant.

So this story of the Big Mill Raid is based only on interviews with Vance and some of his staff and the evasions of Tony Allen.

For the raid on his house Vance has a wonderful start to his story: "About five in the morning I'm upstairs making love to my wife and all of outside the house lights up. So I look through the side window and see all Police cars and vans on the drive and Police vans all up to the top of the road and other vans trying to get off the main road onto Cemetery Road, but they couldn't because there were so many vans already in the way.'

"So approximately two hundred yards of Police vans?"

"Yeah. So I'm thinking – *immediately* – oh my God, someone's been murdered."

"In the street?"

"No I'm thinking I'm being nicked for murder 'cos they're outside my house here. I think like the guy who burned down my farmhouse – and I knew who it was – might have been murdered and they think I done it and they've come for me. I mean, it had to be that or it had to be terrorism. I mean – fookin hell – I just don't understand, what's this all about, so I came downstairs and there was all this screaming and shouting outside, '*Open the door. We're coming through,*' and all that and I'm saying, 'Calm down a minute,' and they're at it, '*Open the door, yah, yah, yah.*' And I'm calling back, 'Calm yourselves down. Until you calm down I ain't opening it, pal.' So he eventually calmed down and I opened the door and – boom – they all came charging in…"

"And grabbing you?"

"Yeah. It was disgusting. And filming it as well – they had fookin' camera crews behind them – camera crews in my kitchen – and the chief copper tried to get me to fight, he really *tried* to get me to fight. And me saying, calm down, you know you're on camera, don't you? I didn't know if they were Police or news cameras, so I said to him, 'Look, pal. The cameras are filming everything you do and you're the one that's getting excited, not me so I suggest you calm down.' Then it was 'On your knees and hands behind your back,' and all that and I'm asking, 'What is this all about?' and they wouldn't say anything."

"They never told you why they were there?"

"Well, I kept saying, 'Will you please just explain to me what this is all about?' and eventually he said 'Fraud – you're being arrested for fraud and I'm bringing you in.'"

Caught up in reliving the event, Vance's voice squeaked up several octaves.

"*Fraud?* Fraud? Who the hell have I frauded? Fook me, it must have been a big fookin' fraud to have caused all this shit."

Eventually he tells me, "You did swap a wooden kitchen cabinet for chipboard," and really, I'm astonished by this. "*What?* All this because you say I swapped a wooden kitchen for a chipboard kitchen? What the fook are you talking about?"

"And how many Police were there? Could you tell?"

"Here. About forty odd plus Trading Standards officers etc."

Vance pauses and shakes his head then says, "It's hard to believe. So they waltz me off, put me in the back of a van and take me to Oldham, throw me in a cell for a day and, regarding the wood for chipboard, they don't even come and interview me. They do interview me about the Quad Bikes – have you read that interview?"

"No. Afterwards I'll have it."

"Yeah. Very funny. You'll love it. I'll give it you. *Extremely* funny."

"Afterward I'll have."

"Yeah. So they don't even ask me any questions. They keep me there all day until midnight and then this copper comes in who led the operation – not the one who gave me all the shit in my house – but another one who's all apologetic to me. He explains, 'Look Vance, this is nothing to do with us, this is not a Police job, we were just drafted in to help these Trading Standards guys so I don't want you to take it personally against us.'"

I interrupt to ask, "Do you have a name? Was it Chief Inspector ****?"

"Yeah, I think it was. And he was really, really sympathetic and said, 'Look Vance, when you get back to your office you're going to have a shock. Everything's gone. We took everything. You've got no phones, you've got no ledgers, you've got no computers and when you get back you'll be on the phone for several days trying to sort your business out.' So he was very apologetic and I got out of jail around midnight and immediately went to The Mill to find every single desk empty. All the desks were cleared, no computers, no pens, no paperwork. No nothing. Empty. They even took all the pictures from the walls of staff families on holiday.

"So they cleared the place out?"

"Yeah. They took all my CCTV. They took all my telephones. And they took all my money. Whatever money they could find they took away. "

"On what basis?"

"Proceeds of crime. And they've still got it."

"How much money did they take?"

"Twenty grand. If they'd have found a million they'd have taken that. And had I any money in the bank they'd have taken that. But at that time I was one point one million pounds in the red with a loan for the China factory, but you can't take an overdraft can you? And that is why they put pressure on the bank to call in the fookin' loan, so I'd go bankrupt and they'd confiscate The Mill. But they couldn't put an order on The Mill because the bank already had an order on it."

"But at this time, apart from the loan, the bank had closed all your accounts?"

"Yeah."

"So how could you pay back a loan if you didn't have a bank account?"

"Oh, God. You should have seen the hassle I had. Although they want me to pay it back they won't allow me to pay money into the loan account. Three times I've been turned away from the bank. No one will accept any money from me. And a few weeks ago they closed down my Euro account in Rochdale. They didn't cotton on to me having a Euro account for a while. When they realised it they closed the account and sent me a cheque for a hundred and fifty thousand Euros made payable to Vance Miller at Maple Industries."

"So you had trouble paying that in?"

"Yeah. I kept it with me for a few weeks trying to open a bank account somewhere but no one would have me, I was blacked. So what am I going to do with it? After a couple of weeks I walked into the bank and said, 'Excuse me, I'd like to cash this cheque please. You don't have to give me the cash now or tomorrow or the day after. Whenever you've got, I'll have it please.'"

"All this was a result of The Mill Raid."

"Yeah. So the girl says, 'It doesn't work like that, you have to put it into an account' and I say, 'But I haven't got an account to put it in to' and she says, 'Sorry, there's nothing we can do about that' and I say, 'Then it's just a worthless piece of paper.'"

Vance's voice rises as he waves an imaginary cheque at me.

"But it says on it – look – Barclays Bank must pay *on demand* the *bearer* of this cheque the sum of one hundred and fifteen thousand Euros. It doesn't say on demand give him another piece of paper. I am here now and I am demanding my hundred and fifteen thousand Euros, please. So she calls the manager who comes out and says, 'Come on, come with me into this room', but I start kicking off in front of everyone in the bank, 'I want a hundred and fifteen thousand Euros but they haven't got a hundred and fifteen thousand fookin' Euros – it's a bank with no money'. And the bank manager gets me into his office and the first thing he says to me is, 'Vance I'm a fan of yours and I'll help sort it out', so I changed the payee to one of my suppliers names and he paid it in and now I'm in credit with my supplier."

I chuckle and say, "So that worked out."

"Yeah but since the guy said he was one of my fans I asked him why I was kicked out of this bank? He said, 'I've no idea Vance,' so I said 'well try and find out for me and a few days later he called me and said, 'As far as we know it was Trading Standards that have been writing to Head Office. Then I phoned him yesterday and asked him was it or was it not Trading Standards that closed down my bank account and he said, 'Vance, I've not heard it personally but my manager told me that Head Office closed it down because of communications they've had with Trading Standards that you are dealing fraudulently and may be money laundering.'"

I think hard for a moment, on the best way to put my next question then ask, "Are you *absolutely* certain you can confirm to me that those words were used?"

"Yeah. Of course I can. Why?"

"When I interviewed Trading Standards yesterday I asked outright if they were involved in the closure of your bank accounts and they said 'No. We would not do such a thing.'"

"Yeah – they covered their arse. They're very poetical and clever. They sent everyone a letter; some worded a little bit different, saying that Vance Miller is being investigated for serious fraud, defrauding and conspiracy to defraud the public for millions of pounds and blah, blah. They sent a letter to everyone I know because they took away all my papers, so they know all my suppliers, all my advertisers. They said 'Send them one of these letters,' and what it is it's a *pretend*, it's a covering their arse 'Oh we're doing our job, we're just asking a few questions, it's just procedure,' but it's not, they're just scaring the shit out of people."

"Have you seen or had access to the bank to discuss this?"

"No. But I've been told they received a letter from Paul from Trading Standards and it's got to be the same one."

"That's enough about that so let's return to the Raid. I understand that the next day your staff came back…"

"Yes. That night I went home and thought it all out – what is the plan, how am I going to do it? The next day I got all my staff in the office and explained that we've got no money, we've got no customers, we've got *nothing*. I bought new telephones and said 'All we will have when I plug all these new phones back in is people ringing us up and saying they've got a problem with one of our kitchens and we have no records to say we ever sold that person a kitchen.' I told them I couldn't even promise a wage at the end of the week because there is no money. I said that those who want to stick with me can stick with me but all I can guarantee is no wage at the end of the week. Those that want to leave – I won't hold it against you. I realise you all have families to keep and mouths to feed so, please, by all means, go and find another job. Do you know, every single person, bar none, stuck with me. They all said, 'Right Vance, we're sticking with you,' so for me it was, 'Right, thanks you lot.' At the end of the week I managed to scrape up half of everybody's wage, at the end of the second week everybody got three quarters wage and by the end of the third week they were all on full wages again."

"And did you then make up the wages they missed?"

"No but they all got bonuses later."

"Someone told me that on your answering machines you directed all calls to Trading Standards. Why was this?"

"Well, we had no paperwork. We were getting people ringing up and saying you owe me four hundred pounds and things like that so we had to take people's word for it. We told them to call Trading Standards and get their paperwork and once we have that we can take your problem on. But Trading Standards refused to give people their paperwork, saying that we still had it and they didn't take all our records."

"Trading Standards actually told people that?"

"Yeah, there are records somewhere of it being said. And they made statements to newspapers they hadn't taken all our records. Of course they took 'em, they took two hundred and eighty thousand documents."

"So Trading Standards were flooded with telephone calls?"

"Yeah, so customers came back to us and said Trading Standards won't give us the paperwork, so we then dealt with their problem – I just had to trust them. Once they'd made a telephone call to Trading Standards, that was enough for me so we sorted out everything from there."

"And did Trading Standards log all those calls as complaints?"

"Yeah, that's why we had one thousand eight hundred complaints that year. I'd like to ask Trading Standards how many of those complaints are still outstanding? And if they tell me 'We don't know,' I'd like to say, 'Well, as a public body, *shouldn't* you know?"

"Someone told me yesterday that eventually, to get all these people off their backs, Trading Standards sent all the paperwork back to you on disc."

"That's bollocks. Oh yeah, they returned them all on disc alright but it was a load of bollocks because they weren't in date order or anything and we couldn't make head nor tail of it."

"So that didn't help?"

"It didn't help one bit. All they did was cover their arse," Vance put on a high class plummy voice to say, "Oh yes, we sent them all back," then dropped back to Lancashire to shout, "Oh yes, they sent 'em back but not in alphabetical order, not in date order, they were in jack-shit order and Mrs Jones's file could be ten per cent on that disc, two per cent on *that* disc and eight per cent of it on that disc and it was a load of discs and where the *fook* do we start?"

"So what you did to overcome this was to call the customers

back and accepted their word and covered their orders?"

"Yeah. Every single one"

"Approximately how many?"

"Oh… around two thousand. I had no choice. And it's a good job we did because we sent everyone a copy of the newspaper articles written that said Trading Standards announced that to minimise the impact they had a team of people ready to move in and take over my company, had I decided to cease trading. What they were going to do was send nobody anything and let everyone put in a claim against us then say, well, we can't finish your kitchen so there are up to two thousand claims and you can claim your full money back, so altogether they'd have about six million pounds worth of claims here; put the company into liquidation and – boom – that would be that."

"I haven't seen those papers but don't worry, I'll get them later."

"It's in The Oldham Chronicle, 30th November 2006 or the day after."

"I'll be able to look that up. To go back to these approximately two thousand people you say were involved with kitchens after the Mill Raid. Of these two thousand, did you receive many complaints once you completed installations?"

"I can't think of any offhand but with two thousand installations there's bound to be somebody not quite happy with something but in general it went ok."

"So it went smoothly?"

"I honoured every single deposit, every single customer was served. This would have been a *fantastic* time to just close the doors. Boom! Right then. If I put that company into liquidation I don't have to service two thousand customers who're in the middle of transactions. I can keep every single deposit that I've taken and have a fresh start. This would have been an ideal position for me to take the piss but I'm not like that."

"Will you use this in your upcoming fraud case?"

"That I could have closed the doors and made all that money? Yeah. It'll be brought up."

"So what did you think of the Mill Raid, later, once you had time to think about it?"

"Well, it was just a publicity stunt and information gathering exercise."

That ended my interview with Vance but I needed more so chatted with three staff members involved at different times during that dramatic day.

Val is a small lady who has worked with Vance for many years in the orders department. She is not used to being interviewed so

I say, "Just tell me conversationally what you actually saw on the day of the raid."

She starts in a quiet voice, saying, "On the day of the raid I got a phone call from Joanne to say don't come in because the Police are all round The Mill. So I stayed at home until half past three when she called again to say the Police had left The Mill and I'm needed in the offices to help because the whole place had been tipped upside down by the Police. She said things had been taken and would I come in to help sort it all out?"

"What did you find when you went to the office?"

"The Police had taken everything, even personal photographs and staff phone numbers off the wall and it sounds silly but we found all the tea and sugar gone. They even took that as well. They cleared the place."

"What photographs did they remove?"

"Holiday photographs and pictures of children and family."

"Have they ever been returned?"

"No. Never. They've never been returned," says Val, her voice rising at such injustice. "So I came in and the whole big office looked as though a bomb had just hit it. In my orders room everything was tipped upside down, drawers turned out all over the floor, paperwork and order sheets just thrown everywhere. There was no need to throw the order sheets everywhere; there was nothing on 'em. I was just amazed, 'cos everything was gone and we couldn't make a brew that evening because, as I said, they'd even taken the tea, sugar and milk."

"So what did you have to do then?"

"Well, we had to clean the place up. It was a terrible mess. Even the rubbish bins had been tipped up. Why did they have to do that? Everything was just thrown all over the place. And the filing cabinets were gone they'd taken those with all the files of order sheets. We keep those for Vance to see how many orders we get in a week and he can tell which newspapers the orders are coming from and if the advertising is working. If a paper is not doing very well, then Vance won't advertise there again. So that's all they got with the filing cabinets."

"So everything went, whatever it was."

"Yes. They just took everything."

"So having cleaned up and returned to some idea of normality, what happened over the next couple of days?"

"Well we couldn't find anything 'cos we'd lost all our paperwork. We had people 'phoning up for deliveries but we'd lost their documents and we had to start all over again."

"Did you tell these people what had happened?"

"Yes. I told 'em that the Police had taken everything but they knew anyway 'cos it was all over the TV. And we had people 'phoning up about the raid and they wanted to cancel their kitchens."

"And did many cancel?"

"Oh yes. There were quite a few people cancelled because of the raid. Our orders must have gone down by about fifty percent, so it was like – where do we go now?"

"Did you have anyone say, 'Oh don't worry, I'll still buy my kitchen?'"

"No, but we talked a lot round to it."

"So of, say, about one hundred, how many did you manage to turn round?"

"About twenty-five percent. It was a big effect on us and took well over six months to start coming back. It took twelve to eighteen months to come back to what we were before the raid. And they didn't leave him alone even after the raid. For months and months they were putting it in the paper and saying what a big bad man he is."

"And as business came back did these new customers know what happened?"

"Oh yes but they said, never mind, I'll still buy a kitchen and we had several who said they admired Vance, because why all them Police officers for just one man? And it was at a business, not a drugs bust or an armed raid – it was nothing. And it was silly at the time. I mean, why *was* it they did such a thing? Anyway, we just stuck at it and for the next six weeks we just went by half pay to help the business get back."

"Is that true?"

"Yes. That's true. We wanted to stick by Vance because he's such a good guy. You know, he'd do anything to help any bugger. And when Vance got back on his feet he made sure we were ok."

"And you got the half pay back?"

"No. We didn't get the half pay back direct but we got a big bonus at Christmas. Not the next Christmas, we got it the one after, because they took all his money. They raided his home as well and took all his money. They took between fifty and seventy thousand pounds and it's never been returned."

"No. Never. And it seems to me that they wanted to put him out of business because they want his Mill."

"Is that your opinion?"

"Yes, it is. They want The Mill. They took over all the other mills round here and think if they can get Vance on something they'll be able to say he's got this mill under false pretences and they can take it off him and sell it. That's my own opinion that."

"Have you any objection if I use what you just said in the book?"

"Oh no. Not in any case whatsoever. You can write what I

said."

"Thank you very much. You've given me plenty to write about, including your opinion of Vance as a boss."

"Oh yes. He's wonderful. If needed I'd work for him for nothing."

"He's not conventional, is he?"

"No. He's not."

Dave has been with Vance from the beginning and has seen all the ups and downs of Vance's life and of the business. His memory of the Mill Raid is very clear; "I got a phone call one morning about half-five or six. It was the security guard who told me to get down to The Mill as soon as possible. He didn't tell me what had happened but from the way he was acting I thought it must have been a robbery. When I reached The Mill I found Police everywhere and the whole place sealed off."

"They were already in the building?"

"Yeah, but because of our positions, me and a colleague, Stuart, were allowed in The Mill. When other staff turned up they were turned away and told the place would be closing and they'd better go and look for a new job."

"Who told them that?"

"Police and Trading Standards – it was feedback I got from

staff turned away that morning. The Police held us downstairs in reception for a while but we were watching them on the CCTV screens and when they saw what we were doing they made us shut down all the cameras while they went through the place. They didn't want any evidence of what they were doing or where they were but they let us into the offices eventually."

"Was it the Police or Trading Standards going through everything?"

"Where we were the Police were alright, we had a chat with a few of them."

"Were the Police going through the files?"

"No. It was Trading Standards going through the files. They weren't reading anything; they were just taking them, collating them, putting them into evidence bags and wheeling everything down the stairs, trolley after trolley. And then they took monitors, printers and everything to do with computers. Monitors and printers have no memory so I don't know why they had to take them. I think they just did it to try and jeopardise the business because you're not going to get evidence off anything like that. They moved us away, saying we weren't allowed to be present and watch what they were doing, especially in the accounts office. Then in late afternoon they said, right, we think we're done and handed The Mill back over to us."

"What did you do then?"

"We got as many staff as we could in to clear up and the following day we got thirty-five to forty kitchens out and delivered to customers."

"How did you manage that without paperwork, everything having been taken?"

"We had some backup records. We got some girls on the telephone. We checked every angle, every little bit of paper that had been left. The reps keep carbon copies of kitchen plans so we just basically started again from scratch. By the end of the next day we were quite surprised how well we'd done."

"So what was it like that day?"

"Hectic. I was running about everywhere – I got a speeding ticket that day…"

"Because you were so pumped up and excited?"

"Yeah, just running about everywhere getting everything organised."

"What about the following, say, six to eight weeks?"

"It was slow and difficult but it picked up and they didn't defeat us."

"They certainly didn't."

"I think their intention was to hinder us to as great a degree as possible, not only for what evidence they needed. There was a lot of stuff taken just to cause us problems."

"And what was the attitude of people who had kitchens on order or who were calling in to place orders over the next several days?"

"Well, after it hit the news we lost some who cancelled but there were others who said we want to order a kitchen because it's good stuff that you've done and, you know, it worked both ways. But yes, we did lose some and the way they did the raid to such a degree was very aggressive and put a lot more people on our side than were against us. But it took a good few months to get back to normal."

"During the day of the raid, were you angry or frightened?"

"Both. I'm a taxpayer as well and to see a hundred and thirty coppers breaking in here made me angry. They don't do that much in a drugs raid. It was right over the top. I don't know why they did it."

Little John is a sort of general factotum around The Mill, helping here and helping there at all times of the day and night. He often stays overnight in the office and was wrapped fast asleep in a quilt on a sofa in the main office when, at five a.m. fifteen men burst through the door, dragged him naked across the room and handcuffed him to a chair.

He says, "I sat there without any clothes wondering what the hell was happening. After they'd chained me up one threw a jumper over my shoulders. The way they were dressed all in black I thought it was a robbery and shouted for Shami our security man. They told me to shut up or I'd be in trouble. They said they were Police and held the door open for another lot to come through who said they were Trading Standards officers. In the end I counted about thirty of them altogether, going all over the office, turning everything upside down and taking it out through the door on trolleys. Some had video cameras and were filming what they were doing.

"After an hour they unchained me and let me go but not before they searched me and all my clothes and took seven hundred and fifty pounds from my bag. It was a customer's money I'd not yet put into the company but they said they were taking it anyway and it has since been returned. At the time they gave me no receipt. Then they let me dress and escorted me out of the office and down the stairs. I was amazed to see the place flooded by Police on every floor, going through the stock and searching for God knows what."

"When I found out later there were over a hundred and thirty of them I thought fookin' hell, there were only thirty on the Soham murders. Why the hell did they need a hundred and thirty for The Mill raid?"

Apart from Little John's quite dramatic experience I heard many similar stories from around thirty other staff involved at differing times through the day. The three included here are representative of the shock, horror and surprise at the enormous attack on commercial premises. Every staff member to whom I spoke expressed dismay at aggressive and quite violent Police tactics. Several asked what on earth were the authorities expecting – an armed standoff?

Not one worker could understand the point of the raid when they heard the reason as suspected fraud. Suspected fraud? One worker said, "Why the hell didn't they just come and ask? We'd have shown them everything."

Local and national newspapers recounted the Raid in suitably breathless fashion, regurgitating most previous wild and inaccurate complaints figures and adding a few. Next day, 30th November, The Oldham Evening Chronicle printed a banner headline shouting WEAPONS FOUND IN MILL SWOOP! The article, written by Richard Hooton, opened with the phrase, "Two firearms have been recovered from Maple Mill as officers search for evidence of multi-million pound fraud against

Oldham's rogue kitchen trader."

Further down the page the article quotes John Rice, an Oldham Council service director at a press conference and mentions the weapons again as being "significant" to the investigation along with computers and paperwork seized. Wording of the article makes it unclear if Mr Rice actually made such a specific statement about the weapons or if the newspaper slipped it in for extra drama. But my search of The Chronicle over succeeding weeks found no mention of the fact that the "firearms" were nothing more than a couple of childrens' toys.

The same article quotes Mr Rice as stating, "Trading Standards had amassed three thousand complaints a year against the company and that the raid took five months to plan." As we know, Trading Standards own figures, obtained under the Freedom of Information Act, show that year recorded only seventy-three complaints. And, according to the same records, no other year shows complaints anywhere near three thousand.

Neither newspaper nor Trading Standards have corrected these two gross inaccuracies – or downright lies. In another telling comment, apparently from Mr Rice, the article says, "If the firm does decide to stop trading then support teams … will be drafted in to help minimise the impact."

This makes Vance and his workers think that the real aim of

the Raid was to shatter their business and take it over to close it down with maximum damage and publicity. The authorities could then justify both the Raid and their oft-stated opinion of continual criminal activity by Vance and his company. However the press conference must have ended on a weak note when Rice admitted to the assembled journalists that he had no power to stop Vance and his business from trading.

What happened next? Not much. After all the rush and aggression of the Big Mill Raid. Vance spent a day in Police cells, subject to only cursory interviews then bailed under Fraud Laws and released at midnight, completely puzzled at why such a raid took place in such a way.

In fact nothing happened until well into the following year when detailed Police interviews took place over the Fraud allegations. Vance and three of his senior staff were then charged with conspiracy to defraud and Vance and one other were charged with twenty-five counts relating to offences under The Trading Descriptions Act. These twenty-five charges were reduced to nine during the next year and after several delays, court hearings were set for September 2009, nearly three years after the Big Mill Raid.

In the same period Vance's business both in Britain and China prospered; expanding and seeing off all competition in every market he serves whilst many of his British competitors shrivelled or went bankrupt. Whatever the eventual result of these charges against Vance, the Big Mill Raid brought him many admirers in the way he took it on the chin and continued undaunted by what they see as shocking Police aggression against a commercial company going about its business. The Police cost of this Raid totalled £7,815.02,[1] which seems expensive for entry into commercial premises freely open to the public during normal working hours.

In a strange side effect of the Mill Raid aimed at possible Fraud, Vance found himself charged with importing unsafe vehicles – Quad Bikes and Mini Mokes.

This was described to me in an interview as, "Trading Standards officers scouring The Mill for something to use against Vance and falling with glee upon some Quad Bikes they decided were unsafe."

This brought further separate charges and a tussle between Vance and Oldham Trading Standards that became quite a caper.

---

1    Source: Freedom Of Information Request

# Chapter Fourteen
## *The Quad Bikes Caper*

For a number of years Vance imported Quad Bikes and Mini Mokes as a successful business venture. He bought originally from Eastern Europe but turned to China as a cheap and easy source, transporting the machines in containers along with kitchen equipment to save transport cost. This added price advantage passed on to his UK customers.

He sold over a thousand machines to satisfied customers without problem or complaint. The Bikes were stored in The Mill to be thoroughly checked and serviced before sale, as with any new motor vehicle. "We never let any Bikes or Mokes out unless fully roadworthy," he told me. "I'd have been daft to allow that and no one ever came back with badly set up machines. We never heard anyone say a machine they bought was in poor condition or dangerous. So about six months after the Mill Raid when the police began to question me about unsafe Quad Bikes found in The Mill I didn't know what they were talking about. They never mentioned Bikes on the day of the Mill Raid"

The day of the Big Raid seems to have been confusing for everyone, with only cursory interviews in police cells. Almost seven months passed from that day in November 2006 before Vance surrendered his police bail to answer fraud charges on kitchens allegedly wrongly delivered. But Trading Standards tried a shock tactic by ignoring fraud and ambushing him – or *trying* to ambush him – about the Quad Bikes.

Vance became furious at the switch and the attempt to catch him out and brought all his big guns to bear on the hapless Trading Standards officers trying to trick him. The resulting interview has been described as a Vance Miller classic. A transcript of the recording appears in the Appendix[1] and is worth reading beyond the extracts I use below. For my account of this interview I modified some phrases used in the transcript to ensure proper flow of reading.

Present to interview Vance were two Oldham Trading Standards officers, John Cassin and Nicola Orbison with Vance's solicitor Alan Neal also present. John Cassin started by going through the legal motions of cautioning Vance and explaining the reason for the arrest and caution.

He said, "You've been arrested today so that questions can be put to you to determine facts surrounding the offences of

---

1    See Appendix 3

possessing dangerous Quad Bikes."

He went on to explain the charges further and made the mistake at one point of saying, "As investigators we're open-minded to all the circumstances surrounding this investigation," and asked Vance to give his version of events.

But before Vance spoke Alan Neal intervened to express disappointment at this ambush and to say, "Mr Miller is here for an entirely different reason this morning." He then went on to say that, despite discussions he had with Trading Standards officials, no indication was given that the Quad Bikes case would be brought up today.

John Cassin said, "Right that point's taken," but before he could speak further Vance took up the attack, no doubt stunning the room with his ferocity. Reading the transcript you can imagine and almost hear the snarl of Vance's loud voice on one side and the startled response on the other.

Vance starts by shouting, "I'd like to say at this point that you've mentioned you are open-minded. Don't talk crap to me. You are not open-minded whatsoever. You are not here to investigate a reported crime; you're here to *invent* a crime aren't you? You're here to find a crime because you want my Mill don't you?"

Vance goes on to detail many reasons why Oldham Trading

Standards have spent years attacking and harassing him and their motive for arresting him and says, "So now I'm going to ask you one simple question. When you've answered my question we'll swap question for question, OK? This is my chance to interview you because I suspect you of conspiracy to steal my Mill…"

He then went on to accuse Trading Standards of lying to the public, lying to the police and lying to the newspapers and asked what he called one simple question, "Why was it you said to the media that I have fifty thousand complaints…when we asked questions under Freedom of Information Act and you could only come up with seventy-three?"

During this tirade Vance said, "If you answer my one simple question I'll then answer your questions. If you don't answer… I'll not answer any of your question. Explain yourselves. Over to you first."

Nicola Orbison said, "Do you want me to explain that?"

Vance said, "Yes please," but John Cassin broke in to say, "Well, that's not the matter we're…"

From the transcript it is obvious that Vance broke in to shout at Cassin, "Are you interfering? No it isn't the matter, nor is these Quads the matter we're here to discuss today is it? The matter we're here to discuss is the fact that I sell people wood and at the last minutes secretly I swap it for chipboard. You're just trying to invent a crime."

Vance went on shouting about the seven months Trading Standards have used to probe his paperwork with their whole office probing to find something, "Well guess what? Seven months later you've got nowt. Nothing. Zero."

I imagine Vance bellowing at the top of his voice that so many officers had searched and searched but found nothing, "So you double the amount of officers looking for nothing don't you?"

Vance ends with a carefully crafted insult, "Don't start telling me, you prick, that you're here…to look at it with open views and all that shit. You're full of crap pal."

John Cassin tries to get back on top but cannot break through Vance's aggressive snarl, "Answer the fookin' question."

Cassin manages a weak, "We haven't made any statement."

Vance shouts, "Fook you prick, answer the question or I'm going out of this room now."

Alan Neal manages, "You're under arrest," so Vance shouts, "Yeah. Well I'm not staying in this fookin' room. Go put me in a cell, I'm not answering any more of your questions."

Vance continues yelling that Trading Standards are here to find a crime and they'll take away whatever he says and look for a crime somewhere. He says, "Go and nick someone that's doing something wrong, go and do your proper job."

He then brings out a few interesting comments on how much money Oldham Council lost last year and shouts, "Why are you the hundred and forty ninth out of a hundred and fifty worst managed councils in the country?" and ends on a telling comparison; "You don't become hundred and forty ninth out of hundred and fifty worst managed councils by doing your job correctly do you? I am the largest independent in the world at what I do. Don't *you*, the second worst at what you do start telling *me* how to run my business, you fookin' half wits."

He then shouts again at Cassin to answer his question saying, "Why did you lie to the tune of fifty thousand complaints down to seventy-three? Go on – why the big difference?"

Cassin's weak response quivers from the page, "We're not here to answer your questions…"

Vance shouts, "Well, are you not? In that case I'm not here to answer yours. Let's go. Give me a room please. Go and have a word with Tony fookin' Allen and tell him Vance said he will answer all my questions but we've got to answer his first. Bye-bye."

With the ambush a complete flop John Cassin – probably stunned by his disastrous result – manages to gurgle, "For the benefit of the tape Mr Miller is leaving the room and I'm switching off the tape recorder."

Vance went back to cells while Trading Standards decided what to do next. Later that day they charged him with breaches of safety regulations relating to the Quad Bikes and bailed him to appear before magistrates on 21st June.

So although Vance surrendered bail in the agreed knowledge that the Mill Raid fraud charges were to be discussed, no questions were put to him about that case until some months later.

Hence Vance's furious irritation at what he saw as a low trick. A lawyer told me later, "The whole day was a sneaky sham orchestrated by Trading Standards who hoped to catch Vance out. But they didn't."

A month later Vance was remanded for trial by magistrates and after several delays and date changes appeared in Manchester Crown Court on 8th December 2008. Not much had happened in the two years since the Mill Raid and the start of Quad Bikes Caper, except that Trading Standards sent in a man described as an engineering expert to compile a report on the state of the Bikes.

The report claimed problems such as a loose screw, an improperly marked on/off switch, an unguarded chain, a dangerous fuel pipe, faulty brakes and steering, improperly vented exhaust and insecure batteries. It also suggested footrests near the engine could cause heat injuries to legs and suggested danger from an unguarded chain.

After two days of legal argument the case went before a jury where, on the third day it collapsed when the defence cross-examined the prosecution's engineering expert. He agreed that under normal practice, Quad Bikes are prepared for sale by being thoroughly serviced, checked and tested and that the derogatory points he made against the Bikes would be fixed in that service. Under cross-examination he conceded the Bikes were not unsafe and did not contravene safety regulations

During the case Vance's defence barrister dug out a series of answers from Kevin Welch, a Trading Standards officer on actions and attitudes to Vance and the Quad Bikes: -

"Did you receive any complaints about the Quad Bikes?" "No."

"Are you aware that many types of Quad Bike have no chain guard?" "No."

"Do you have any previous experience of Quad Bikes or Quad Bike prosecutions?" "No."

"Did you seek to recall any previously sold Quad Bikes from customers?" "No."

"Why not if you considered the Bikes unsafe?" "We just didn't."

"Were you present when your expert tested the Quad Bikes?"

"Yes."

"Did he drive or run one to check engine heat?" "No."

"So it was only a visual inspection?" "Yes."

"Are all these actions with the Quad Bikes designed simply to put Mr Miller out of business?" "No."

After two requested adjournments the prosecution offered no further evidence. The judge instructed the jury to find Vance not guilty on all charges and awarded full defence costs.

This first Trading Standards attempt at a result from the Mill Raid turned into a bitter defeat for the Oldham authorities. Councillor Mark Alcock is quoted in Oldham Evening Chronicle as saying "I am extremely disappointed. The collapse of this case has left Government backed safety standards with a gaping hole."

My research could find no Council comment at a gaping hole in Council pride caused by what seems to have been an inept and unwarranted prosecution.

Other comments include one in Manchester Evening News of 17th December: "Bosses at the cash-strapped council who are looking to cut 543 jobs have refused to confirm how much the failed prosecution cost."

Perhaps the best and most cutting remark came from Vance, quoted in The Manchester Evening News when he "Slammed Oldham council" and said, "When are they going to stop wasting taxpayers' money on me? It wouldn't surprise me if they tried to invent a new law just to say that black socks are illegal because I wear them."

Another amusing aspect of those three days in court saw Vance striding the corridors during every recess, whispering into his mobile telephone. MFI, Britain's largest retail kitchens company went into administration for the third and final time on 20th December 2008, Vance's second day in court. Vance the serial entrepreneur spent every spare moment for three days, first trying to get hold of the Administrator, then arguing and offering and doing his best to buy the bankrupt company, all in an urgent hiss.

He failed to buy the company, "Beaten to it by some bastard," but a few days later bought the complete stock of MFI kitchen doors at knockdown prices and set up a Web Site called mfikitchendoors.co.uk. So anyone who entered MFI into their search engine jumped straight to Vance's bright new doors, all laid out in elegant colour and excellent prices. He also set up an MFI customer care website to direct any queries in the right direction.

All this whilst on Crown Court trial with a possible prison term in the next few days. This must be the true mark of an entrepreneur able to assess and take risks and damn the consequences.

# Chapter Fifteen
## *Slings And Arrows*

The slings and arrows of outrageous harassment could paraphrase Shakespeare's famous line in relation to Vance.

Such a heavyweight barrage of legal and media ordnance slung at Vance over so many years would have destroyed most men. The psychological pressure must have been immense, but Vance survives and prospers, cheerful and progressive. He rides out every storm and remains afloat and confident.

"How?" I ask him.

"Because I'm doing nothing wrong. The bastards are out to get me although I'm doing nothing wrong. Every time I've been arrested I ask them to tell me why. I offer to answer all questions but they don't ask any. I'll cooperate with anything to help them see how my business is run."

Following the collapse of the Quad Bikes prosecution, in a brilliant stroke Vance wrote to Oldham Trading Standards suggesting a meeting to discuss what they wanted of him and how they could advise him to improve. This he did with the Big

Fraud Case against him in September 2009 in mind. This case appears to be based on whatever evidence of fraud came from the Big Mill Raid in 2006 and a second similar Raid in January 2009.

Vance saw his request to meet as helping him with the Big Fraud Case. If Trading Standards accept, Vance shows the court his willingness to cooperate. A Trading Standards refusal would show intransigence and a lack of willingness to work face to face for improvements. At the same time he offered to allow a Trading Standards officer to work full time in his business, all expenses and salary paid by Vance. With full access to all workings, papers and functions of the business over a long period, including direct contact with customers, an officer would soon discover any fraudulent trading.

Vance could not resist a gentle dig at Oldham Council's financial problems. He wrote, 'I understand that Oldham Council will be making redundant in excess of five hundred people in March. Maybe this would be a fine opportunity to save one or two of those jobs with my suggestion'.

To Vance's delight, Oldham Trading Standards replied and agreed to meet but stated it would have no impact on the outstanding fraud case. They also set out a series of conditions and requirements and suggested an action plan on how to proceed.

Vance agreed to the conditions and replied with a few points of his own, including a dig at The Advertisings Standards Agency for criticising his description of solid granite as "solid granite" and instructing that the phrases real wood and solid wood should be referred to as "wood effect". Vance points out that this wording describes something *not* made from real wood.

Before going to a first meeting Vance set in train some of the Trading Standards recommendations and wrote asking for advice on others. The first meeting went well in a polite and co-operative atmosphere and settled down to regular consultations of apparent value to both sides.

This partly shows how Vance can act under the pressure of harassment that started in 2001 and continued almost non-stop since. The first major legal attack by Trading Standards came through a new EU law known as the Stop Now Order. This is aimed at traders thought to be acting illegally with customers and gives regulatory powers when a court is satisfied that a trader has engaged in conduct *or is likely to* engage in conduct that infringes the law. This complex piece of legislation, which appears to the layman to be deliberately vague, requires the trader to stop the infringement.

The law seems aimed at the individual not the company and in Vance's case Trading Standards satisfied the court that Vance was, at that time, misrepresenting goods and delivering kitchens of either the wrong materials or failing to accurately deliver every part of a specific kitchen order.

Vance absolutely denies misrepresentation at any time but agrees it is possible to short-deliver the several thousand parts that make up a modern kitchen.

He says. "It's easy for one of my men to miss out a couple of door handles or hinges in a big delivery but they are always sent later. So I can break this law just by getting out of bed in the morning and doing nothing else. I'm to blame for someone else's mistake."

The Manchester Evening News of 27th July 2001 reported the possibility of action against Vance in a long article that included a list of his previous convictions – none relating to the kitchens operation – and included critical comments about Vance running his business from the gym he owned. This article also named Vance "Kitchen Rogue", a title that stuck ever since.

The same newspaper reported the Stop Now Case and Vance's conviction in December 2001, quoting that Vance's business received "…a very large number of complaints," without specifying a figure.

Media pressure increased during 2002 with a Manchester Evening News report of 15th April stating that seventy-five percent of customers complained to a value of kitchens worth three million pounds. No source is given for the accuracy of this report and I could find no such incidence of customer complaints in Vance's business records. As already shown, complaints officially recorded by Trading Standards in the year before that date amounted to only eighty-three.

Similar inaccuracies appeared in various newspapers and other media, recycling the same dud figures as though fact, leading to Vance appearing on a number of television programmes such as Rogue Trader and Watchdog. This form of harassment continued throughout 2003 and 2004 with my detailed research finding nothing accurate or supportive of Vance until the BBC2 documentary *Notorious* in 2002, showing Vance in a better and uncritical and more accurate light.

In the making of this programme Vance at last found a media friend in Alastair Cook, the documentary maker. He spent a lot of time with Vance during filming and in a later Internet posting supporting Vance he said that the style and manner of wording used by Oldham Trading Standards to mention the programme is designed, '… to mislead readers into believing that the programme showed Vance Miller in a bad light when it, in fact, shows quite the opposite.

Alastair goes on to say, 'I found Vance Miller to be likeable, fun to be with and extremely hard working but above all I found Vance to be the most honest business man I have ever met.'

The full statement posted by Alastair[1] in August 2007 was too late to have any effect on the increasingly hysterical Press and official harassment of the previous four years from 2003.

In April 2004 Customs officials at Manchester Airport stopped Vance from boarding a flight to China and confiscated £66,000 he was carrying to pay Chinese suppliers. Newspaper accounts tell of the action in detail, saying it is unclear whether Vance was targeted or stopped as a routine check.

The money apparently seized under The Proceeds Of Crime Act designed to target drugs dealers and money launderers, was returned a few weeks later and no charges brought. I hunted but found no comment on this U-turn in any newspaper.

In June 2005 Vance was banned from running registered companies until 2014, so switched status to Sole Trader and carried on.

In a possibly crippling action the Vehicle Licensing authorities cancelled all Freight Vehicle licences for Vance's business. Vance went out and bought a fleet of smaller vans and carried on.

Newspapers and Trading Standards wrote articles and leaflets asking readers to call or write to complain about Vance and

---

1     See Appendix 4

his business.

The local Vehicle Inspection authorities appeared early one morning to set up weighbridges at exits from The Mill and spent several days delaying deliveries by weighing every loaded vehicle. Vance and his staff just shrugged and carried on.

The Mill Raids and arrests failed to stop the business. As already described, Vance and his staff rode the blows and carried on.

Vance's house and farm were burnt down in arson attacks and local newspapers implied a "gangster" link, without specifying what sort of gangster. According to Vance the police showed little interest. Although Vance gave them names no arrests followed.

In May 2007 Vance and his staff ambushed and captured a couple of alleged armed raiders entering The Mill. Based on his experience of the police attitude to arson at his houses, he held the raiders overnight for interrogation. Vance was later arrested and charged with kidnapping the raiders. A few days later the charges were dropped and Vance fined £80 for 'wasting police time.' No investigation of the alleged attempted armed robbery occurred, confirming Vance's opinion of the police attitude to him, to the safety of his staff and to his business.

Newspapers and Oldham Trading Standards; headed by Tony Allen, continued Press and Public Relations attacks on

Vance and his business. In July 2007 Tony Allen issued a Press Release warning of possible fraud in dealings with Vance and his company. As we have already seen, at that date no fraud of any kind had been proven against Vance.

In fact during the same month an implied fraud case against Vance's business failed before Deputy District Judge Boora (Peaty v Kitchens) in the Stafford County Court. A few weeks later the Oldham Advertiser reported local Trading Standards as stating Vance's business had brought them "No recent complaints in the Oldham area."

In another possibly crippling action during December 2007, Barclays Bank closed all Vance's accounts overnight, leaving him completely without banking facility because no other bank will take on a business in such circumstances. Vance simply bypassed the banks in several ways and simply carried on as a cash business.

In May 2008 Vance was fined £90,000 plus £30,000 costs for breaking his Stop Now Order. This judgement is under appeal but in a significant comment reported in Bury Times, the judge "Rapped the Office Of Fair Trading for their skewed evidence and cooking of the complaints figures."

This is the first and only official comment I can find that implies Trading Standards are not precise, direct and truthful in their dealings with Vance.

So despite years of pressure plus a judicial comment that Trading Standards may be harassing Vance unfairly and two court cases lost (Quad Bikes and Peaty) the authorities continued to act in a manner that could be construed as persecution.

Two journalists from different Manchester area newspapers agreed to be interviewed. Both have written exaggerated stories about Vance over the years and both hold private personal regard for him in the way he has survived. During separate interviews both implied agreement with Vance's opinion that his ownership of The Mill may be a factor for the years of authoritarian oppression. In vague language they inferred The Mill is at the centre of an area of regeneration that Oldham Council probably want cleared of old buildings. Whether this is true or not, it seems to be a definite opinion among the majority of non-council people I interviewed.

Vance's survival and business skills have brought admiration on the Internet in a backlash of support. Several independent chat or blogging sites show almost equal measure in support and criticism. A good example is Blagger.com that carries some vitriolic posts giving Vance and his company a hard time. Yet in the period from March 2008 to January 2009 in the forty-seven posts shown, twenty-five are complaints and twenty-one praise and satisfaction. One post comments that the praise comes from

Vance's staff and friends who have not bought kitchens. Another comments that some of the complaints are by Council staff and business competitors who have not bought kitchens either.

A very interesting Blog site is Ukpreneur.co.uk, which, over a long period has watched and mainly admired Vance. Some rude and critical comments appear but these are outweighed by carefully considered comment and analysis.

Christine, an American television producer comments, "After wading through quite a few interesting articles on 'The Kitchen Gangster' I'm convinced that Mr Miller is living in the wrong country. I say this because his business tactics and relentless pursuit of opportunity in China would render him nothing short of rock star status here in the US business landscape."[2]

Most interesting is a long analysis by Mark Assheton of the legal aspects of the Trading Standards attacks. In a long article he suggests that Tony Allen and Trading Standards are contravening a number of laws and statutes and breaching the Data Protection Act in their pursuit of Miller. He comments that in 2007 when he wrote the article Trading Standards were not listed in the Crime And Disorder Act as authorised to disclose information to other agencies such as the police, so their sharing of confidential data should lead to prosecution.

---

2     See Appendix 5

He then goes on to comment that Trading Standards have widely publicised falsified numbers of complaints in a premeditated and lengthy campaign to malign Vance Miller. He refers to a 2004 report written by Tony Allen stating that well-established informal arrangements to exchange confidential data between unauthorised departments sound fine but could end up in court. Mark Assheton suggests that Vance should issue summonses against those authorities and individuals and asks where have the significant funds come from to pay for the massive campaign to ruin Vance Miller?

Such support in mid-2007 seems not to have been followed up by Vance or bothered the authorities who, in January 2009, mounted a second Raid, apparently looking for the same evidence of fraud.

# Chapter Sixteen
## *The Second Mill Raid*

At dawn on Sunday 11th February 2009 a force of around seventy Manchester Police officers threw a second large Raid at The Mill and Vance's house.

Manchester Police again refuse an interview to explain the purpose of the action and the number of officers used to enter commercial premises and a private house in such heavy-handed fashion, so this is another one-sided account.[1]

Enormous press publicity attended the First Mill Raid in October 2006, with journalists and television cameras pre-warned and on site ahead of the Police. This gave maximum print and picture coverage with almost the whole UK press shouting quite hysterical stories for days and weeks.

A strange and absolute silence attended this Second Mill Raid. No word appeared in local or national press, or on any television or radio news channel. I tried to uncover this odd silence by asking a well-known Manchester newspaper reporter

---

[1]     See Appendix 6

why no big story?

He'd heard of the incident and tried to follow up but been warned off by the authorities and told to keep quiet. Why? "Legal reasons. It may affect the case they're trying to set up against Vance, " he said. "No PR release, no pictures, no interviews and nothing to be written on anything to do with this Second Mill Raid."

I ask, "Why keep so quiet after such a hullabaloo two years ago? The big fraud case is soon. Could it be they found no evidence in the 2006 Mill Raid and are panicking?"

He shrugs and says, "Perhaps. They've had over two years to go through all the paperwork confiscated then and it seems peculiar they needed another run at it."

My meeting with Vance to hear his part in this story took place in the bedroom of my hotel because of his fears of electronic bugs at Cemetery Lodge. In great pain from a long-term back condition he lay on the big double bed with my recorder bouncing and jiggling each time he moved to ease his discomfort.

Few staff work on Sunday so accounts of what happened in The Mill that day are sketchy but again Vance woke to racing engines and the bash of boots on gravel and batons on his door. He says, "It was exactly the same as the First Mill Raid except with seventy coppers instead of a hundred and thirty. So it was the same situation and the same time but on a Sunday morning at about a quarter to six. They must have been paid overtime. They came into my house and stayed all day but this time it was a bugging exercise, wasn't it? They came to bug my home, my offices, my car, etc. So eleven officers spent something like eight or nine hours in my small two-bedroom house. What would eleven people do in such a house if they weren't bugging it? It's beyond me. I've had some bug detectors in to check where they are."

"You weren't there all that time. They took you away and put you inside."

"Yeah. It's pretty medieval really, that they can just bust into your home, lock you away and rifle through all your personal items and bug your house to death."

For the first time since I met him, Vance sounds depressed at what he sees as continual unfair pressure aggravated by the extreme and continuing back pain of the last few months.

"Did your bug detectors find anything?"

"Yeah. And we found a house by The Mill with a window facing my office with all bugging equipment in. Our detectors showed the rays were all coming in through the window."

"They're bugging you from outside? Or have they put bugs

inside your office to transmit to the equipment in the house?"

"Yeah. Bugs inside transmitting to outside."

"Do you know where they are placed?"

"Not yet but we have a guy coming at the weekend to find and remove them from my house and office."

"Are you absolutely sure those places have been bugged?"

"Yeah. We know there are bugs but we won't know how many until the guy's been next week. When we use the telephone we can hear what we say repeat itself as it goes out the window. That's why we're here now, sitting in this hotel room."

I end this rather rambling conversation by saying that I'll check later how many the sweeper finds.

Vance lapses into silence, staring at the ceiling, probably reflecting on the nine days he spent in prison after this Second Raid. I can understand some melancholy or mild paranoia but have never seen Vance affected by such deep gloom despite far greater problems in the past.

I break his silence by asking, "What happened then? They took you to the police station? Did they question you?"

"Well, they started to but I told 'em to fook off and leave me alone in my room. I wasn't going to be questioned that day."

"What did they have to question you about?"

With a heavy sigh Vance says, "Exactly. They don't

question me to *investigate* a crime. They question me to try and *find* a crime within my words. If they find a crime within what I've said then that's what they'll charge me with. But there hasn't been any crime."

His mind wandered to past problems. "Without some words from me they haven't got any crimes. So then they changed the crime element. First of all they went for swapping wood with chipboard and when they realised my chipboard was really wood, they…"

"Hold on. Go back over that. Be more specific."

"When they raided us first in 2006 the original charge was that I swapped wood for chipboard."

"And how do you think they found your so-called chipboard was truly wood?"

"Well, they investigated it, obviously. Then they changed the rule that because a door is pieces of wood joined together I'm not allowed to call it solid wood. Well I never called it solid wood, I called it real wood."

"And is that still a charge?"

"Yeah. It's still a charge but because they're on weak ground with that one they've now, from this Second Raid, introduced a new charge. Just in case they lose the wood for wood, the new charge is that I sell and deliver a product that – without them saying what it is – is not as good a quality as I say and after advertising and selling it I'm then delivering a product that's less quality."

"And that's worth being in prison for nine days?"

"Oh. And another new charge is that I've conspired with others to hold back information that I had a legal duty to disclose about who was operating our company, Rock Solid Kitchens. Even my solicitor says he's never heard of such a charge in his life."

"And how did that come about? At what point were you ever asked to disclose that information?"

"I don't have a clue. The VAT number is registered in Alan's and my names so how can they say I *conspired* with Alan to say it was his company, not mine?"

"So this was the reason for the Second Raid?"

"Yeah. After I sat in police cells all day they let me out then a few days later I was arrested and put in jail by a magistrate and they took my passport away."

"Have you got that back yet?"

"Yeah. The Crown Court returned it when they let me out after the nine days."

"And was anything taken from The Mill in this Second Raid?"

"Yeah. But not everything like last time. This time they seemed to be more about deciding what to take. They took a great deal of paperwork but nothing near the amount they took first time. That first time they weren't very educated and didn't realise that taking away two hundred and eighty thousand documents would be a big thorn in their side."

"Did they take money again?"

"Yes, they took money. They took forty two thousand pounds and gave us a receipt for ten. They said they hadn't counted it yet and estimated it as ten and that's all the receipt you're getting."

"Do you have a record of that money?"

"Yeah, but you can't prove anything about these people, they could put everything in their pocket and give me a receipt for sixpence. I then wouldn't be able to prove it wasn't sixpence."

"How much did they take in the First Raid?"

"Around sixty five to seventy thousand."

"And you would hope to get it all back after the upcoming fraud case?"

"Yeah. This whole thing is just to make my job difficult."

Vance seemed to have nothing more to add so I leaned forward to switch off my recorder…

Because The Mill was more or less deserted that Sunday I later took a telephone interview with Juanita, Vance's Personal Assistant.

Juanita is a smart modern young woman. She is an actress and works with Vance between parts. Her cheerful nature and optimistic attitude brighten everyone at The Mill and she works all hours, often seven days a week, to look after Vance and his business. She takes a central role in much that happens in and around The Mill so those staff present on that Sunday kept her regaled by telephone with confusing continual updates of what was going on around them.

Juanita says, "My telephone rang about six thirty early Sunday morning but I ignored it. When I listened to the voicemail about nine thirty it was a chief of the Greater Manchester Police asking if I had a key to the cash office in The Mill? I called back to say no but by that time they'd already called a locksmith and broken in. I then called Joanne, one of our staff, to find out what was happening and she said The Mill had been raided and staff were being turned away from the door, same as last time."

"So although it was a Sunday, staff came in to work?"

"Yes, such as members of the appointments team and some others. Joanne told me that Vance had been arrested and a warrant is out for Alan's arrest but they hadn't caught up with him yet. So Vance was out of touch and I spent my whole day trying to find out what had gone on?"

"So you never went to The Mill?"

"No. It seems thirty or forty police went to Vance's house and another lot went to The Mill so I was trying to get hold of Alan and find out what the situation was and why it was all happening. I managed to contact Vance's solicitor but he knew nothing about it, so he got straight on to the police to try and find out what had happened."

Reliving the day, Juanita's voice rose and speeded up to almost a high pitched gabble.

"We didn't know for the rest of the day what had happened. With everyone calling me my 'phone was really busy all day. Vance's Mum wanted constant updates and I didn't have any. I finally got hold of Alan. He said until he knew why they had arrested Vance he was pretty reluctant to go and turn up at the police station. So we knew he was alright and round and about but that he wouldn't be coming to The Mill. Then later in the day Vance's solicitor started to get information that Vance had been arrested for pretty much the same as the last time round and, again, it was Trading Standards led."

"So you didn't go to The Mill on Sunday?"

"No. I went in on Monday and we were supposed to have

guests that day from Ireland and when they rang up I didn't know whether to tell them to get on the ferry or not. I wasn't sure if I should tell them Vance had been locked up again."

"It could have been very embarrassing."

"Yes but in the end we decided to tell them to come over and arranged for someone else to look after them while we found out what the situation was with Vance, although I do recall that Vance was let out on Sunday at around nine in the evening. The following day we all turned up at work as normal and it was a bit weird because we were trying to find out what had been raided and what hadn't. I found that my desk had been bust open and prised open and stuff was missing with certain sections and pages taken from certain files. So they hadn't done what they did the first time and taken massive quantities of paperwork but they'd been selective about what they took. All my files were still there but they'd obviously gone through every page of every folder and my laptop was gone too."

"So was Monday just a day of tidying up or did the Police come back?"

"Well I then had a call to say the Health And Safety people were here but that turned out not to be true because they were more police. In any situation like that in The Mill, Vance wants a recording on film, or at least a voice recording so he can't be accused of things that aren't really true. So I asked Darby to do that and stay with them and film whatever they were doing. The next I heard was that three of them came up into the office. They were very obnoxious, very rude and very loud."

"Were they in uniform?"

"No. I actually think now they were the tougher side of the police, the ones that genuinely threaten to smash your face in when nobody's looking, which is basically what they'd done to Darby downstairs. They pushed him up against the wall, taken the camera off him and more or less said that if he tried to film them again they'd take him in a room and batter him. Then they came upstairs and shouted at me for telling him to film because it was hindering their Bobbies. I was very surprised by their manner. I've never seen police behave like that. They were – I don't know really – a bit unprofessional. More like hooligans than police."

"So the Raid ended on Monday?"

"Yes."

"Vance told me that he thinks they came to bug the office and he found a house opposite where the police were listening from. Did anything happen about that?"

"No. A few days after the Raid Vance and I stayed late checking with a little machine he has."

"What, a bug finder?"

"Yes. He thought he detected signals coming through a window from a house opposite. Next day he went to the house that seemed to be a bit of a hot spot and asked but nothing came of it."

"And did the bug sweeper find any bugs in the office?"

"No. He said that the tests came back clear."

"So you have no evidence that the police tried to bug the buildings?"

"No. None. But if they weren't there to bug I can't see the point of the raid. They covered our CCTV cameras with sheets but not very well so you could see their feet and they stood for a long time round the big desk. They didn't come to remove stuff en masse like the last time so they obviously came with a specific purpose. Their main focus was our accounts office and what they took ties in with what they took from my desk – anything to do with the company financial information as opposed to orders."

"Vance told me they took money from the accounts office. Do you know how much?"

"We believe about forty thousand. But I don't think that figure has ever been confirmed by them."

"Vance says they gave you a receipt for ten thousand. Have you had a receipt for any more money since then?"

"No. I don't believe we have."

That ended my interview with Juanita and it seemed to me that the question of bugging might be in Vance's imagination and part of the reason for his gloomy mood that night in the hotel. But I remembered that at the end of my earlier interview with Vance, in a sudden change of mood he launched the story of an interesting sequel to his nine days in jail.

# Chapter Seventeen
## *Local Hero*

At what I thought was the end of our hotel interview about the Second Mill Raid I leaned forward to switch off my recorder, saying, "Well I guess that's about all," when, in an abrupt change of mood Vance sat up, waved his arms and almost shouted, "Whoa! Wait! Hang on! One other thing did happen."

His gloom vanished. He became animated and pointed for me to sit back and listen. "A rum story about me when I came out of prison."

"When? This time?"

"Yeah. They turfed me out around seven at night with nothing. I came out with these Asian kids and they had a car so there were five of us in this little car but we were squeezed in and I couldn't stay in the car any longer so I told 'em to let me out, let me out. We were in the middle of Swinton. They'd pushed me out of jail with just four pounds in my pocket so there I was on the street with only four pounds and no telephone. My bad back was killing me and I just wanted to lie down. I was frozen

– it was the coldest night of the year so far, about minus seven, apparently – so I started walking and walking, just walking along and wondering what the hell I was going to do? I walked for about half an hour then this bus came along…"

"And what day was this?"

"Friday. It was Friday night. So I ran after the bus and jumped on it and found it was going to Bolton so I jumped off and carried on walking and after a while I came to a pub. It was an old grotty looking pub a bit like walking into The Rover's Return, you know, the pub on Coronation Street when Annie Walker used to run it. It was like going back in time. So I walked in and asked if they had a telephone? So the woman said, 'Yeah, over there, where have you come from?' so I said, 'I've just got out of jail, love,' and I must have looked it 'cos I'm unshaven and whatnot. So I bought half a pint and I'm down to three pounds now and I went to the 'phone and started to get people phoning me back and then I took my shoes off and went to lie down 'cos my back was really absolutely killing me."

"What did they think of that?"

"Well, I lay down with one foot on the chair and one on the floor and the landlady came and started telling me off, 'What do you think you're doing?' and all that and I'm saying, 'I've not got my shoes on,' and she's going 'Well I don't care and blah-blah,' so I stood up and started walking up and down and rubbing my back. And everyone in this pub is looking at me, the landlord's looking at me and the people in there are looking at me walking up and down, all unshaven, no shoes and rubbing my back. They're looking at me as if I've escaped from jail and whatnot. It must have looked funny.

"So I thought I ought to write about this so I asked for paper and a pen and stood at the bar writing about this experience of getting out of jail. Everyone was looking at me and I could hear all this whispering round the lounge and the landlady comes over to me and says, 'You're not called Vance Miller are you?'"

At this point Vance giggles in delight at the memory of being recognised.

"So I say yes I am Vance Miller and she says, 'Oh sorry love. I'm so sorry I told you to take your feet off the chair and whatnot,' and I said, 'Don't you worry love, it's not a problem.'"

"Why did she change?"

"Well, this is why I wrote about that night, how unbelievable, how *unbelievable* it went. How a man that just got out of jail with only four pounds in his pocket and everybody looking at me as if I was a sinner and a nothing and I was worthless, to all of a sudden how I was the hero of the pub. Everybody was buying me drinks, giving me cigarettes and I was the *hero* of the pub…"

"Because they knew of you."

"Exactly - because they knew of me. And what I was… what they saw me as and what they portrayed me as…is the man who fights the law and wins. That's what they all consider me. They were all going on about how great I am, giving the authorities a hard time…"

"So they saw you as a local hero?"

"Yeah. All of a sudden with these people I went from nobody to being their hero. Nothing changed apart from – all of a sudden – they knew who I was. So my name made such a difference between being a nobody and being a somebody."

"Was that it? Have we finished with the Second Raid or is there anything else?"

Vance thought for a moment and said, "No. I think that's it. But wait…"

He brightened up again and launched another story.

"While I was in jail the Deputy Governor came to see me and said I was the most famous man on the criminal circuit in Manchester."

"So he knew who you were."

"Yeah. All the screws knew me and three of the screws in there used to work for me and several of the cons in there used to work for me. And my cell was bugged."

"How do you know?"

"They told me. When they were booking me in…"

"The screws?"

"Yeah. They said, we're not telling you anything Vance but the electricians have been working in your cell all morning but they still haven't got that light working."

"So what else did the Deputy Governor say when he came to see you?"

"He came into the cell and said 'Hello Vance. I know all about you,' so I said 'All right, what do you know then?' and he said 'I know you can be difficult when you want to,' and I said, 'You've just got me completely wrong,' but he was just coming to make peace, really, just to say I know you can cause trouble but I want you to stay on our side while you're in jail. But he judged me all wrong – he thought I was like one of the Kray twins moving into his jail."

"He doesn't know what a pussy-cat you really are."

"Exactly. But I was the most famous kid in there. Everyone was demanding to see me. I was getting requests to move onto different wings, so people could see me. Some of the kids had mobile phones and were saying come over to our wing and you can use our phones if you want. It was crazy."

"On this subject of being famous – do people recognise you on the street in Manchester?"

"Yeah. In Manchester but especially in Rochdale where I can't even get out of my car."

"And people give you support?"

"Yeah. Everybody knows I'm not a villain and I get plenty of respect. Only people who don't know me well – people that have only heard of me – give me some respect because they think I'm a gangster. But people who get to know me see I'm not a villain. They know I'm far, far, far from being a gangster. There's not anyone in Manchester I've ever met who really thinks I'm a gangster."

I mulled over this rather muddled statement and decided to leave it to lie, so asked, "Is there anything else you want to say before I close down?"

"No. Not really. Only that it was shite being in jail again but now I think back, it was nine days that I wouldn't have gone without. I'm glad I did it."

He half closed his eyes and grinned, probably remembering the pleasures of fame even in prison and when apparently destitute. This change to good mood stayed while we called for a car, walked down to the lobby and waited. Before he got into the car he gave me a big hug and said, "You're a fookin' nuisance whenever you come here with all these questions. But I like you."

The car drove off and he waved. I stood feeling a moment of loneliness because – apart from the big court case soon to come – my book is finished. No more interviews. No more entrancing stories. No more of this man who has been in my head most waking hours for well over a year.

# *Epilogue*

As author I avoided giving any hint of opinion when preparing and writing this book. I also refused to answer when many times asked what I think, replying always "I have no opinion. At least not until the book is complete and published."

To hold or express opinions would have disabled my neutrality and probably slanted interview questions to suit a prejudice for or against the several sides involved.

However, it is difficult not to sympathise with Vance and the enormous pressure experienced over eight years. In addition to all the official, legal and media attacks on his business, he has seen two of his houses burnt down, lost large amounts of money to armed raids against his business, been chased by Police on trumped up charges, seen his mother's home attacked and fought a great blaze that destroyed half of Maple Mill.

Despite all this his business bounced back each time to flourish and see off all competition whilst watching competitors shrink or disappear into bankruptcy. He is one of the largest employers in Oldham and is honoured and feted in China where he maintains the livelihood of whole villages by one means or another. One section of The Mill is given over to storing classical stone and plaster figures of the sort seen in Italy and Greece. "What are they doing here?" I ask Alan, Vance's long time colleague. "Oh, he found a village in China that made these but couldn't sell them and felt sorry for the people. So he keeps the village going by buying most of their production and importing it here for sale."

Most of the story I have written is based on the drama of complaints and attacks on Vance and his business. But it is interesting how much unreported support Vance receives, ignored by the press. A good example is a nasty, waspish, petty piece in the Daily Mirror Blog reporting The Mill fire in April 2009.

The fire started in a generator outside Mill 2, used for storing and manufacturing kitchen parts. Sparks appear to have jumped to pallets nearby, causing flames to heat up and explode a number of gas cylinders. The six-storey Mill 2 caught light and burnt down, collapsing in a pile of rubble and Victorian steel girders. By luck the majority of those working inside were at a meeting in Mill 1. The few still inside got out at speed without injury of any kind.

The scurrilous Blog comment by Penman and Sommerlad says, "We never like to see a factory going up in smoke but in the case of Vance Miller's base in Oldham…

The dots are presumably a sort of nudge-nudge to imply they

are really very happy that Vance faces such a catastrophe because the piece continues with sniping at their twisted perception of Vance and comments, "…it looks like his kitchen empire has come to a sudden end."

The piece shows pictures of the two fearless journalists, glowering at the camera and captions Andrew Penman, Editor, as starting the Sorted Investigations column in 1997.

Ah yes. "Sorted". The column that "investigated" Vance on so many occasions and seemed sure they would put him out of business is wrong again. They failed to spot that although the Fire Brigade withdrew after a fairly short attendance, leaving the pile still burning, Vance led his staff in a superhuman effort for several weeks to control and douse the remaining danger while at the same time continuing business from Mill 1.

A few weeks after the fire I walked round The Mill with Alan and inspected the terrible damage. He told me they lost millions of pounds of stock in the blaze but within a few days brought in enough parts to continue manufacture and showed me a completely rearranged Mill 1, now an efficient, fully racked store holding and delivering kitchen parts with hardly any interruption. "In fact," he said, "We're delivering more kitchens a week than before. People called in to say they wanted to help and buy kitchens from us if we could supply. So the fire seems to have done some good."

And here is an interesting point. This Daily Mirror Blog also contains comments from readers worth seeing because almost without exception they are supportive of Vance and his business and extremely rude about the two fearless investigative journalists. Some come from customers who bought Vance's kitchens and are happy with the result. One comments that the reporters are disgusting and childish for showing pleasure at such disaster. Another from someone living near The Mill mentions Vance's work ethic, "I see Vance Miller arriving at work every morning before I leave and he is still there when I get home. I also see him working at weekends so if he were a conman like you say, then surely he would find himself a con that took up less of his time…"

These are different views of Vance seldom shown by the media. During my research I came across a letter from Susan Pratt who lives in Buckinghamshire. In 2007 she said she had been to The Mill with her husband and liked what she saw. Then, following a chance conversation she researched Vance and saw all the negative news about him and his business and accusations of fraud. The letter goes on to ask if he is honest and will he let her down if she buys a kitchen?

Finding no written reply from Vance I telephoned Susan

and asked what happened next? I was lucky to find a bright and intelligent woman well able to stand up for herself against local authorities in several contests.

Susan told me, "Before that letter my husband called Manchester Trading Standards who told him they had numerous court cases pending with dissatisfied customers. Basically, they blackened his character right left and centre and, actually, I'm not sure I've ever come across such a personal opinion in such an official position ...I think, basically, they should have been more careful what they said about him. So I wrote to Vance and a few days later he rang my mobile and chatted and gave me a personal guarantee that all would be well, he sent me everything written about him and the television programmes on DVD so I could make up my own mind. Seeing the programmes I was more than impressed with the way Vance runs that operation and more than impressed that he took the trouble to ring me himself. Seeing the Rogue Traders programme, the worst it seems to me that Vance could be accused of is that some of the deliveries didn't meet the customers' expectations with pieces missing or broken. But I believe Vance took that on board and did something about it. I can't see how that constitutes fraud in any way, shape or form and the only way to describe this, really, is victimisation."

In our interview, Susan expressed surprise at the way Trading

Standards are handling Vance and said that in her experience of tradesmen, Vance, came down as a really minor problem to anybody." I can tell you that twenty years ago I ordered a kitchen from Magnet that gave me so much trouble with wrong worktops that took six weeks to fix and there was nothing I could do about it. There must be more complaints against people like Magnet and MFI previously than there are against Vance and nobody takes a blind bit of notice.

"When I saw the television programmes, especially *Brits In China*, it made me think of teams of bureaucrats sitting around in meetings achieving nothing and, I know it's his own company so he has a reason to be efficient, but he just made things happen, which there is too little of these days. As soon as a problem occurred he wanted to get at it, sort it and move on. And I thought that, in spite of the swearing, I thought he was excellent and I'd like to put him in charge of The National Health Service. In fact, I'd vote for him as Prime Minister

We both laughed and I said, "Well, Susan, you're not the first who's said that about the Health Service and someone on the Internet has already suggested putting him up for Prime Minister."

"Really? Well perhaps we wouldn't be in the mess we're in if we did. I can't bear inefficiency and I just thought he was top dog in getting things done."

In the event Susan did not buy a kitchen from Vance because she decided Oldham is too far away from High Wycombe but she remains a Vance admirer.

It is surprising how many people who have met Vance – including some local journalists who write about him – find him entirely different to the public perception often brought about by the articles they write. I asked one well-known Manchester reporter, "In the pieces you write why do you always refer to Vance as 'Rogue Kitchens Trader?' You did it again last week when the piece seemed quite innocuous."

The reporter chuckled and said, "I called him 'Controversial Businessman' but it was subbed out."

"So the sub-editor replaced your description with Rogue Trader?"

"Yes."

"Because 'Controversial Businessman' was not controversial enough?"

"Yes."

It is difficult for the outside observer to understand much of what is said officially about Vance. During my tour of The Mill with Alan he spoke of recently being in court, preparing for the upcoming Big Fraud Case against himself and Vance. Alan told me, "In the corridor I said to one of the Trading Standards officials, 'Why are you doing all this? You know that we employ over two hundred young Oldham men and if they weren't working for us, most of them would be on the streets robbing. If we are closed down and put them back on the streets you'll be unsafe to leave your office.' And the guy said, 'Yes, I know'"

In the same conversation Alan told me of an armed cash raid on him as he left The Mill carrying seventy-five thousand pounds cash in a bag. A female employee telephoned to let the waiting gang know when Alan and his bodyguard started down the stairs. The robbers rushed forward waving a gun and a samurai sword, shouting, "Give us the money."

The bodyguard, faced with a pistol, froze but Alan – a small, tough bundle of muscle – leapt to hit one of the raiders and with a swing of his arm tossed the bag onto a nearby roof. Unfortunately the bag caught in the gutter, held for a second then dropped back onto the road. Alan and two raiders dived for it and in the fight that followed Alan, literally fearing for his life, received several severe cuts from the sword and, scrapping as street fighter, shoved one raider back with such force they both smashed through a plate glass window. A long shard stabbed into Alan's shoulder causing massive injury, taking Alan out of the fight.

Eventually force won and the robbers raced away in a car

with the money, leaving Alan shocked and bleeding but with pictures on his mobile to show when describing the raid. Despite one of the robbers probably bleeding badly no one was caught and the money never recovered. With no direct proof the only action against the female employee was dismissal. Alan showed contempt for the way the Police handled the case and feels sure if the robbery had been on any other company more would have been done to investigate and arrest the gang.

Another story Alan told of perceived victimisation refers to Vance's support for Stefan Kisko, wrongly jailed for the rape and murder of Lesley Molseed. Alan said that the Manchester Police were angry with Vance for leading a long campaign to release Stefan due to insufficient evidence.

Alan said, "We were in a Mill in Rochdale at Vance's gym with about a couple of hundred people to fund raise for that guy wrongly imprisoned, Stefan Kisko and Police came and busted the place and arrested me and Vance."

"Why?"

"To stop the function going on because the Police didn't want that making any headlines. So they arrested Vance and me and charged us with grievous bodily harm on the police. When we went to court and my case came up they had about twenty odd Police there as witnesses against me, telling what happened at the incident but because I was a fundraiser they dropped all the charges. The judge said, 'What are you doing? These men were raising money for charity ' and we all walked out of court."

"When was this?"

"About two years ago; 2007 I think."

"The guy was still in prison then, wasn't he?"

"Yeah. He was still in prison. We were trying to raise money to get him out. The Police were terrible. They fought us and bounced us off the back of vans. It was unbelievable. It was crazy."

I am told that Vance supports a number of charities, especially those that benefit children and teenagers but beyond saying that, none of his staff will speak of it. I tried to dig information on this from Vance in one meeting but he refused to tell me anything. "It's just something I do," he said.

"But why not let people know?

"Who'll believe it?"

This is true. Most people only know Vance from a hostile media with no interest in spoiling the great story they have largely invented with help from certain authorities. Another example is the glee in reports of The Mill Fire hinting quite broadly that it must have been insurance fraud, the inference being, "Here he goes again."

What shattering disappointment to hear Vance tell one

reporter "Not insured, pal. They won't insure me. The Mill's too old so we've never been insured." You can imagine the tooth-gritting frustration in some newsrooms at the loss of a juicy story.

None of this implies I am breaking my neutrality rule. I am simply reporting what I am told and commenting as an outside observer.

One last example of the Press Effect on Vance's business, told to me by an ex-member of The Kenya Police whom I met from having also been in that superb force. Through my research I met him and we had much to discuss of our days in Kenya. I turned the conversation to Vance and my friend came out with an interesting tale.

He said, "I got a contact from my son who was contemplating buying a new kitchen. He'd seen this firm's advertisements on the Internet or wherever and because I live in Oldham asked if I'd visit the premises and give him a report on what I thought of the units being advertised. I went with my wife and looked at the units and we were very impressed with them; they looked really, really good. We got a very nice brochure and sent it to my son. But then the storm broke around this firm and we were quite deterred – quite considerably – by the enormous amount of adverse criticism that came up over the quality of the units concerned."

"And the storm that broke and description of quality of the units was what you read in the Press, rather than your own opinion, having *seen* the units?"

"Yes, because the units we'd seen on display seemed to be of very high quality. But all the many bad reports on television and newspapers and conversations in our area have not done the firm any good."

"So you are saying that neither you nor your son would have purchased from Miller's business because of the adverse media stories and the conversations that they brought about?"

"Certainly I think that stuff in the media does have an effect. It certainly had an effect on me and I would certainly have been deterred from any sort of purchase."

"I find that very interesting because although you saw the quality of what is on offer the general media attack would have put you off buying from this company."

"It would. Certainly."

So. That is almost the end. One last story remains: The Big Fraud Case. Vance is defending himself on the basis that he knows more about his business than anyone else and can expertly refute all charges thrown at him. This means he has been out of contact for the past two months working from dawn to the small hours every day with Juanita and his legal team, going through the thousands of pages of prosecution evidence being passed to him.

This first week of September 2009 we await the Trial that starts on 14th. I intend to break a chronological rule and place the Verdict *after* the Epilogue. Not for dramatic effect but because I think it will give a more rounded picture of Vance than almost everything else I have written.

## Chapter Eighteen
# *Trial And Verdict*

The Big Fraud Case opened on 14th September 2009 in Manchester Crown Court at Crown Square before Judge Jonathan Foster Q.C. Prosecution lawyers had four years to prepare. Vance, defending himself before the jury, had only three months during which the prosecution bombarded him with around twenty-five thousand disclosure documents.

To survive this onslaught Vance cut out the world. Locked in his Maple Mill office from dawn each day until two or three the following morning, he refused all outside contact. Immersed in an atmosphere of intense concentration and frequent extreme anger, he spoke only to snarl orders at Juanita, his personal assistant. For those three months Juanita worked the same hours alongside Vance, hunting down and feeding out files and documents at his snapped commands.

Near the end of this period Oldham Council sent Vance a schedule of their office and investigation costs between 2006 and the day the case opened, amounting to over two million pounds. Vance quickly saw the document as a ruse to unsettle his concentration and self-confidence during this critical period. To get this money Trading Standards needed to win their case. His close study of prosecution disclosures revealed a twisting of evidence, including the leading of witnesses during statements in order to reach a conclusion suitable for prosecution, along with direct lies and forgery.

The trial opened with the original twenty-three charges reduced to twelve then to three, with two main charges of conspiracy to defraud referring to advertising kitchens as being made from "Solid Wood" or "Real Wood" and substituting with inferior materials. Alongside Vance in the dock stood Alan Ford, Nicola Brodie and Sadiya Hussein, the two ladies being included in the conspiracy to defraud. The third charge of conspiracy by failing to disclose information on the ownership of their companies included only Vance and Alan.

The planned two days legal argument without Jury lasted two weeks. Although Vance intended to defend himself before Jury he employed the legal expertise of a barrister, Mr Jim Pickup, for this difficult period. He also employed three other barristers, one each for his co-defendants, causing repetition of evidence throughout the trial. A strongly argued defence point suggested that refusal by the Judge to include new charges at an earlier hearing indicated a weak prosecution case, "hanging on by its fingernails."

This contention may be vindicated by the fact that twice the prosecution offered Vance a plea bargain; the first a few months previously and again just before the trial started. Vance said to me,

"Not a hope. Why should I plead guilty to something I've not done to save them from calamity and big costs?"

Jury finally came in on 28th September. Vance transferred from dock to defence bench and Mr Pickup departed. The Judge immediately ruled the case as based on real wood/solid wood, stating peripheral matters such as handles, doors, hinges or granite, irrelevant.

The prosecution barrister's opening speech contained a comment that, "During the Mill Raid in November 2006 officers found no sign of wood cutting machinery or the manufacture of real wood kitchens." This caused surprise to those who know Vance's business. Could it be that Trading Standards evidence gathering is so inept they did not understand that all Vance's wood kitchens are imported from his own Chinese factories and suppliers already cut and shaped? As the case progressed this slipshod approach to prosecution evidence and witness statements became more obvious.

Prosecution intended to call around twenty-five witnesses, including customers and Trading Standards officers. Most came to court in good faith and willing to give honest replies. Many agreed under cross-examination that Vance's company satisfied their original complaints one way or another, usually within several days. But some witnesses entered court with clear malicious intent to lie or do Vance personal harm.

One, an old man named Wheatley, seemed at first oblivious to his own deceit before eventually agreeing that he had ordered a £2,300 kitchen then changed the figure and forged a receipt for £12,300, the amount he demanded when returning the kitchen as being wood veneer, not the solid oak ordered. He also telephoned Vance and offered to buy his company for one pound, saying, "When you come out (after this case) you'll be broke because you'll have nothing left."

Another, a well-dressed and well-spoken woman from Scotland appeared at first to be quite pleasant, complaining that her kitchen was not what she ordered and did not suit the stable style cottage in which she lived. She also implied that the kitchen contained non-wood parts, insisting that the kitchen, although still in use, did not meet her standards as being "Not what I had in mind." Under detailed cross-examination by Vance she seemed to become increasingly waspish and spiteful. Forced to accept that an independent surveyor reported the kitchen as being good quality and made of wood she kept repeating, "But it was not what I had in mind." She confirmed that Vance made personal contact and offered to visit Scotland and ensure her satisfaction, had offered to change the kitchen at no cost, had offered to remove it and give her full repayment. But she kept spitting out, "That's true but I didn't want you or any of your staff anywhere near my house," so destroying early sympathy she may have gained from the court.

Then came a witness named Brian Manning who, in 2006, took employment as a kitchen salesman with Vance's company. Being led through his statement by the prosecutor he could not remember the town he went to for a three day training course, could not remember who conducted the course, could not remember which kitchens he trained on, could not remember actually seeing any kitchens, could not remember his salary and commission details, could not remember the name of the company he had joined. Even the Judge intervened to lean forward and ask, "Did anything interest you at all?" Explaining he had been hunted down by Trading Standards to give his statement, the witness explained a discrepancy by saying that the interviewing officer added words to his original draft statement.

He told the court, "I didn't say that," remarking that the officer later removed the extra words as being unsuitable for the final statement now before court.

A number of Trading Standards officers from round Britain gave mostly innocuous evidence, apart from one who boasted ability to detect laminates from real wood by a "knock test" that entailed rapping the wood with his knuckle. Offered two doors by Vance he failed on the first, stating, "laminate" with confidence when testing a real wood door. To chuckles in court he refused to test the second. Another officer stated that The Mill Raid briefing contained no instructions to search for wood so they went in "…just to take anything." He also said, "On the raid we were also wearing body armour…" When laughter in court subsided the defence barrister asked, "To raid commercial premises and homes? Weren't you embarrassed?"

Then came Daniel Moore who, in addition to duties as Vance's main Oldham Trading Standards contact for many years, arranged and attended The Mill Raid. During almost five days of cross-examination Mr Moore showed the astonishing inefficiency with which his department prepared for The Raid. Defence barrister Mr Jim Gregory asked if analyses of sales and purchase documents were examined to show what products were bought and sold? No! Were containers examined to check if products imported were mainly wood or laminates? No! Was anyone with wood, kitchen or accounting experience employed in this investigation to check financial documents, which make it obvious that plenty of wood came into The Mill? No! In obvious frustration Mr Gregory asked, "What on earth were you doing during this investigation?" adding, "In truth this investigation was an exercise in bad faith."

Vance took over cross-examination and asked why Moore did not come to The Mill for a chat in October, a month before The Raid? "Your call caught me by surprise and The Raid was in full planning." Over many hours Vance kept digging and laid bare the obvious ignorance and lack of knowledge that Mr Moore and Trading Standards had of his business, underlining several times that no officer ever visited The Mill to check what products were stored and sold. Vance asked, "During The Raid did you know where (to look for) solid wood in The Mill?" "No!" "Why Not?" "Because I did not believe it existed."

This answer, an admission of brainwashing and implied incompetence, brought a gasp throughout the court. A lawyer later said to me, "Trading Standards only believed what they wanted to believe in their aim of trying to bankrupt Vance."

At one point during his cross-examination of Daniel Moore, Vance dropped his voice and in a moment that struck me of extreme sadness said, "Mr Moore. You've never given me a chance."

Vance then produced a letter relating to a complaint Vance made to the Advertising Standards Authority about B&Q the large kitchens company advertising Chipboard as Solid Wood. Laughter in court accompanied the Judge's incredulous question, "You made a complaint?" In the letter B&Q apologised for "the mistake" and Vance insisted that Daniel Moore read a current B&Q advertisement still advertising Chipboard as Oak and asked, "Have Oldham Trading Standards taken any action? No! Why the different treatment, Mr Moore?"

The next Trading Standards witness, Kirsty Robinson, described as senior investigating officer for The Mill Raid, immediately stated she took hardly any part in Raid planning until 19th November 2006. On that day she saw a letter dated in mid-July confirming her new status. Vance asked if she had any say in whether The Raid went ahead? No! Did you know of any detail relating to The Raid? No! Did you make contact with anyone at The Mill (to obtain detail)? No! The Judge commented, "So you knew something was going on but you were not involved." Yes! Kirsty Robinson also repeated several times the Trading Standards mantra that she did not believe any solid wood was present in The Mill. To avoid delay at one point, the Judge suggested that going through piles of documents to show stock of wood doors purchased, imported and delivered could be shortened because, "…Prosecution evidence is weak on details of The Mill Raid and evidence so far (before the court) makes it obvious that plenty of wood is in The Mill."

The poor woman spent several days struggling in the witness box, her evidence underlining not only the haphazard nature of the investigation but also how Oldham Trading Standards ignored their own Risk Assessment guidelines that calls for many inspection visits to High Risk traders. Vance asked if, in the months and years before The Raid she knew of any inspections at The Mill? No!

The final Trading Standards witness, Tony Allen, head of Oldham Trading Standards and prime mover in The Raid and the case against Vance came to the stand for what turned out to be a marathon session of many days. He first endured forensic questioning by the three Defence barristers, including Jim Gregory who brought out that Tony Allen appeared ignorant of what materials were in The Mill both before The Raid and after, when reviewing confiscated papers. Under pressure at one point Tony Allen appeared to blame the prosecution barristers for the choice and standard of evidence being presented in court. Mr Gregory said, "You would say anything and are driven by personal animus against Mr Miller…You abjectly failed to properly investigate what was in The Mill. You have a closed mind…to the presence of wood." Later in his evidence Tony Allen stated that he alone made the decision to press charges. He also said to Jim Gregory, "I would like to have closed the business down and that remains the case," and repeated the Trading Standards mantra that he did not believe real wood existed in The Mill.

At last on 15th December Vance faces his main tormentor in court where questions must be – or should be – answered straight and honest and true. Sixteen weeks observing and conducting detailed cross-examinations have turned Vance into a confident and fluent advocate. Armed with deep knowledge of his kitchens business and the months of pre-trial work and concentration he is poised and ready.

He takes a deep breath and asks if Tony Allen's assertion in an internal Email that, 'Should all assets be seized it would make it difficult for him (Vance Miller) to continue,' meant the intention of The Raid was, to close me down? No!

These words started four days of cat-and-mouse exchanges that gave detailed insight into many aspects of Tony Allen and his Oldham Trading Standards operation. Vance went straight for the throat by saying, "I'm going to prove over the next few days that you're an expert at misleading and a liar."

Vance then started digging and digging at Tony Allen, examining his actions, his logic, his state of mind and ability to do his job. Here sat the man who, for eight years, in Vance's eyes, has harried, bullied, oppressed and with gross abuse of power tried to bring Vance and his business to ruin. He firstly exposed Tony Allen's lack of solid information by showing a wooden door and asking how many wooden samples had been seized during The Raid? The answer: "I don't know. Not many." Vance says; "Oh, lets guess. Five? Three? Er, how about ...none? Zero?" Tony Allen's answer: "If you know how many, then none."

Vance gets into stride and taunts Tony Allen: "Carry On Trading Standards, have you seen it?" The answer: "No, I must have missed that". Vance leaps, "But how? Didn't you pay £3 million pounds for the ticket? What were you thinking? It's like 'Beavis and Butthead go to The Mill' Hey Beavis, did you bring the wood back? ...Duh, no, I thought you had it." During earlier evidence Tony Allen used many quite meaningless management phrases that Vance now reads out, including, Strategic analysis, Tactical assessment, Target profile, Operation command suite, Gold commander; Covert human operative. Vance comments, "Sounds like a military campaign (but) this is about wood, isn't it? Kitchens?" At one point the Judge spoke to say, "Mr Miller, I understand you are angry, but these are just cheap shots and you have better points you can make."

A long examination followed during which Tony Allen stumbled through a confused explanation of complaints figures used to justify The Big Raid. Finally the Judge intervened to ask, "Did you know the (complaints) figures in the tactical assessment were wrong?" Discussion followed between the Judge and Tony Allen on collection and accuracy of the figures, with Vance and Mr Field, the prosecution barrister chipping in. During the exchanges the Judge commented, "Maybe this is double Dutch!" Finally Tony Allen admitted inability to understand some of the data he used and that he lacked confidence in the figures at the time of The Raid. Vance jumped in to say, "So you launched a three million pound Raid on this?"

Tony Allen's evidence went wandering along, frequently vague and several times contradictory. One light moment occurred when Vance queried why Trading Standards engaged Sue Carver, described as a wood and furniture expert. Her role, for a fee of £22,000 was to attend the first Mill Raid and, according to a report in the Oldham Chronicle, to inspect kitchen furniture found. In the event, without proper instruction, she made her way through several floors and, according to the Chronicle reported the cabinets she inspected could be 'reasonably described as solid wood.' Ms Carver was not called to give evidence and her report was not presented to the court but Vance had studied a copy and asked Tony Allen. "When you read (the report), did you feel something running down your leg?" To loud general laughter throughout the court, one barrister left the court in an apparent choking fit.

Tony Allen's vague and sometimes contradictory evidence ground on until 23rd December when the Judge took Vance and the four barristers into Chambers and told them privately his ruling that the case would go no further. When Court reconvened on 12th January before a crowded gallery, the Judge published a thirteen page Final Ruling.

"No Case To Answer" on the Conspiracy To Defraud charges and agreement from the prosecution that the Conspiracy To Defraud through misuse of the Business Names Act could hardly stand-alone.

Judge's comments throughout the Ruling read as a damning indictment on Oldham Trading Standards methods and Tony Allen's inept conduct of the whole investigation and condemning Oldham Council for bringing a case that was 'misconceived from the start'. He called The Big Mill Raid disproportionate and oppressive, saying he had also considered the phrases, 'heavy-handed and overzealous (but) they did not sufficiently describe the operation.'

In a direct personal comment on Tony Allen's initial desire to close the business down the Judge added, 'I find that I am unable to rely on his evidence.' He listed reasons, including misrepresentation; contrast in evidence to the court between September and December and a loss of objectivity so he did not give a fair and balanced approach to the case. His many other comments cover details of general incompetence and inefficiencies in the gathering and handling of evidence and the two Mill Raids. (Read the full report in Appendix 7)

Within minutes of the court rising, press and media fell upon the story with glee. Their spotlight turned to Oldham Council and Tony Allen questioning what cost to the Council and what next for Tony Allen? Oldham Council kept silent but figures between four and five million pounds appeared in the press. Oldham Council decided not to appeal and said, "We are disappointed by the Judge's decision but this was an extremely complex and ground-breaking case." They made no mention of their own silly conduct in allowing a farcical case to go ahead. Nor any hint of apology to Vance and his staff for years of harassment, oppression, libel and slander now uncovered by the court.

What next for Tony Allen, mastermind and main mover behind for the whole incompetent mess? Suspension from duty, reported by Mike Keegan in Manchester Evening News of 13<sup>th</sup>

January, so what follows could be serious career damage and possibly the sack.

And what next for Vance? Back to work…

# Epilogue 2
## What Happened Next

The end of Chapter Eighteen, entitled Trial And Verdict, ends with the question "What next for Tony Allen?"

I should have asked, "What next for Tony Allen and Oldham Council?" so for this first reprint I break the rules and write a second Epilogue on what happened next with both.

Immediately following the collapse of their case Oldham Council suspended Tony Allen from duty. This may have been due to a litany of criticism from the Judge as reported in Manchester Evening News (MEN) and The Oldham Chronicle, which included misrepresentations to the Office of Fair Trading, lack of objectivity and proper evaluation and alarming inconsistency and contradiction in his evidence to the court and that he could not rely on Tony Allen's evidence.

Oldham Council fared little better in the papers with even the quality broadsheet Daily Telegraph reporting on 13th January that the "flawed prosecution" would cost the public £5 million. Alarmed politicians and members of the public flooded MEN and Oldham Chronicle with acid comment on the lack of intelligence and supervision of Oldham Council in respect to the failed and costly prosecution with bloggers on the newspapers' sites calling for resignations and action against the "Muppets" involved, especially Mr Charlie Parker, Oldham Council chief executive. Some of these are worth reading on MEN and Oldham Chronicle websites by entering "Vance Miller" in the news search box and going to the bottom of the news reports. In response Oldham Council set up an "independent review" chaired by Mr Dobson, described in the newspapers as a lawyer with 32 years of local council work.

During February interviews with both MEN and The Oldham Chronicle Tony Allen tried to publicly absolve himself of blame for the failed prosecution, saying that the case failed not because of his investigation team but because the courts did not take allegations of consumer fraud seriously and that the council prosecuting team did not 'present the compelling case that it was.'

May 2010, the suspended Tony Allen lost a high court request for a judicial review of Judge Foster's "severe criticism" that 'ruined my career.' According to MEN he told the court of 'pressure on Oldham Council to use me as a scapegoat,' and that the Council must try to find something to justify summary dismissal. In early August both papers reported his dismissal by Oldham Council although this may not be Tony Allen's last shot as he immediately announced an appeal and possible legal action, which I suppose will be against the Council.

As for Vance, he returned to the Kitchens business and newspaper reports that, in his usual cheeky fashion, he offered Oldham council a deal – that they give him their old and dilapidated town hall, abandoned in 1978, to turn into a leisure facility for the young people of Oldham. In return he'd consider not seeking further recompense from the Council. No report appeared of acceptance so in addition to recouping his legal costs, Vance is no doubt preparing a large bill for damages following eight years of Council harassment and serious disruption and loss to his business.

So the Vance bandwagon rolls on. And I'll bet we haven't heard the last of him.

# Appendix 1
## *Oldham Trading Standards Complaints Analysis*

## *Chief Executive's Directorate*

---

Mr J Newton

**Your reference:**
**Our reference:**     AE/PRO1/149
**Please ask for:**     Alan Evans
**Direct Line:**     0161 770 3019
**Fax No:**     0161 770 3701

**Date:**     19th December 2007

Dear Mr Newton

### FREEDOM OF INFORMATION ACT REQUEST

I write with reference to your request under the Freedom of Information Act relating to the number of complaints received by the Council in relation to Mr Vance Miller and his company based at Maple Mill, Cardwell Street, Oldham.

You will recall that I indicated to you that the Council could not provide you with any information about Mr Miller unless he gave his consent. I have now received a letter from Mr Miller giving me permission to release to you the information about his companies.

I have set out below the number of complaints received by the Council in relation to Mr Miller and his various businesses.

1st January to 31st December 2001 – 80 complaints, 49 service requests

1st January to 31st December 2002 – 249 complaints, 366 service requests

1st January to 31st December 2003 – 185 complaints, 328 service requests

1st January to 31st March 2004 – 60 complaints, 66 service requests

1st April 2004 to 31st March 2005 – 138 complaints, 320 service requests

1st April 2006 to 31st March 2007 – 1853 complaints, 868 service requests

1st April 2007 to 30th November 2007 – 566 complaints, 53 service requests

A complaint is where someone is making a specific allegation and a service request is where someone wants advice or information about a subject, but is not making an allegation.

Prior to December 2005, complaints could be made to either Oldham Council, as the home authority for dealing with complaints in relation to Mr Miller's companies or to the Trading Standards Department for the area in which the complainant lived. From December 2005, an organisation called Consumer Direct has handled all consumer protection complaints from across the country and forwarded them to the appropriate home authority to investigate and deal with. Many of the service requests forwarded to the Council prior to the introduction of Consumer Direct would have been complaints, but have not been recorded as such by Oldham Council to avoid the same complaints being recorded twice – once by the originating local authority and once by Oldham Council.

The Council is unable to provide you with any comparative complaint statistics relating to other organisations. The Office of Fair Trading holds this information but details have been provided to the Council. Section 44 of the Freedom of Information Act prohibits the disclosure of information where its disclosure is prohibited under any enactment. Part 9 of the Enterprise Act 2002 imposed restrictions on the disclosure of specified information which relates to the affairs of a business or undertaking. Specified information includes information which comes to a public authority in connection with the exercise of any function it has under various statutes, including the Trade Descriptions Act 1968. Such information must not be disclosed while the undertaking continues in existence (section 237). The information you requested is held by the Council pursuant to exercising its functions under the Trade Descriptions Act and therefore Part 9 of the Enterprise Act applies to it and it cannot be disclosed, pursuant to section 44 of the Freedom of Information Act.

If you disagree with the Council's decision not to provide you with information about the comparative complaint statistics, you do have a right of appeal. Please write to:-

Aileen Johnson
Director of Legal and Democratic Services
Oldham MBC
PO Box 33
Civic Centre
West Street
Oldham
OL1 1UL

Should you further disagree with the decision following the appeal, you may wish to contact the office for the Information Commissioner as follows:-

Office for the Information Commissioner
Wycliffe House
Water Lane
Wilmslow
Cheshire
SK9 5AF

I hope that the above information is of use to you.

Yours sincerely

**For Solicitor to the Council**

C:\Users\John\AppData\Local\Microsoft\Windows\Temporary Internet Files\Content.IE5\0VN9CYCP\letter to Mr Newton re FOI 17.12.07.doc        3

**Mike Chambers,** Deputy Chief Executive & Director of Change
**Aileen Johnson,** Director of Legal & Democratic Services
Civic Centre PO Box 33 West Street Oldham OL1 1UL  Central Switchboard 0161 770 3000
DX 710000 OLDHAM - Civic Centre www.oldham.gov.uk

<u>Complaints Analysis</u>

National and Oldham Total Complaints April/(July) 2008

<u>OFT National Figures</u>

OFT Letter shows 3491 complaints as set out below

July 2004 to 31st December 2008 = 53 months = 216 weeks

    3588Complaints during period
      66Complaints per month
      17Complaints per week

<u>Oldham Trading Standards Complaints Figures For Similar
Period</u>

April 2004 to 30th November 2008 = 55 months = 220 weeks

    3362Complaints during period
      61Complaints per month
      15Complaints per week

<u>Difference</u>

    3588National complaints figure
    <u>3362</u>Oldham complaints figure
     226Difference being complaints complaints nationally outside Oldham area

These official figures indicate that complaints from the rest of Britain are neglible.
On average only four complaints a week generate from outside the Oldham TS area
Does this indicate that the local pressure on Miller and his company result in excess complaints?

*Kitchen Gangster?*

Monthly/Weekly Average Complaints

Complaints Through Oldham Trading Standards

|  | Per Year | Per Month | Per week |
|---|---|---|---|
| Jan - Dec 2001 | 80 | 7 | 2 |
| Jan - Dec 2002 | 249 | 21 | 5 |
| Jan - Dec 2003 | 185 | 15 | 4 |
| Jan - Dec 2004 | 60 | 5 | 1 |
| Apr 04 - Mar 2005 | 138 | 12 | 3 |
| Apr 05 - Mar 2006 | 73 | 6 | 1 |
| Apr 06 - Mar 2007 | 1,853 | 154 | 36 |
| Apr 07 - Nov 2007 | 566 | 47 | 11 |
| Apr 08 - Nov 2008 | 158 | 13 | 3 |
| Total for 7.75 years | 3,362 | 76 | 19 |

Source - Oldham Trading Standards Letter 19th December 2007
Note: April 2006 to November 2007 covers period affected by Big Mill Raid

National Complaints Including Oldham

|  | Total | 53 Months | 216 Weeks |
|---|---|---|---|
| Jul 2004 - Dec 2008 | 3588 | 66 | 17 |

<u>OFFICE OF FAIR TRADINC</u>

Mr John Newton

Your ref

Our ref       EPIC/ENQ/L/21482

Date          16 January 2008

Direct line   (020) 7211 8801

Email         Ian.Bennett@oft.gsi.gov.uk

Dear Mr Newton

**REQUEST FOR COMPLAINT INFORMATION REGARDING MR VANCE MILLER TRADING AS 'KITCHENS'**

I refer to your letter of 18 December 2007 in which you request:

> "the nation-wide incidence of complaints against Kitchens and Vance Miller that came through Trading Standards"

You will appreciate that the OFT would not normally give out personal information to a third party However, we note from Mr Miller's letter dated 11 December 2007, that he has provided you wit permission to request and receive what amounts to his personal information.

Although your request for information has been made under the Freedom of Information Act 2000 (FOIA), in view of the fact that Vance Miller is an identifiable individual trading as Kitchens and th permission given by Mr Miller referred to above, we are dealing with your letter as if it were a request for 'personal data' from Mr Miller himself. Such information is exempt under section 40(1 of the FoIA, and we are therefore treating the request as a subject access request under section 7 of the Data Protection Act 1998 (DPA).

In relation to numbers of complaints against Kitchens "made through Trading Standards", please note that the OFT does not, strictly speaking, hold such information. However, we can confirm that a total of 3491 complaints against Kitchens had been received by 'Consumer Direct', coverin the period July 2004 to 31 December 2007.

As you may be aware, Consumer Direct (CD) is a national consumer helpline which provides first tier advice on a range of consumer matters, including information on consumer rights and practic guidance on individual complaints and how to gain redress. CD launched in Summer 2004 in

INVESTOR IN PEOPLE

Office of Fair Tradin
Fleetbank Hous
2-6 Salisbury Squar
London EC4Y 8J
Switchboard: (020) 7211 800
www.oft.gov.u

Scotland, Wales, Yorkshire, Humber and South West; expanded to cover the South East, London, East of England and East Midlands in June 2005; and went nationwide in April 2006.

You will appreciate therefore that, prior to April 2006, CD complaints recorded would not (to varying degrees) include complaints made in all parts of the UK. You should also note that a small number of local authority Trading Standards Services still continue to provide equivalent first tier advice to consumers in their areas. As such the figure above also does not include complaints from consumers who have contacted these authorities directly.

During the same period, the OFT received 286 written complaints about Kitchens. Please be aware, however, that some of these complainants may previously have contacted CD, and will therefore also be included in the CD complaint figure referred to above.

If you wish to complain about the way in which your request for information has been handled, you may seek an internal review by writing to:

The Internal Review Co-ordinator
Room 4C/046
Office of Fair Trading
Fleetbank House
2-6 Salisbury Square
London
EC4Y 8JX

We will deal with your complaint within 25 working days of receipt or, if this is not possible, advise you of a date by which we expect to have completed a review of your complaint.

If you remain dissatisfied with the OFT's response you have the right to complain to:

The Information Commissioner
DPA Complaints Resolution
Information Commissioner's Office
Wycliffe House
Water Lane
Wilmslow
Cheshire
SX9 5AF

Your sincerely

Ian Bennett
Data Protection Act Coordinator
OFT Information Access Team

OFFICE OF FAIR TRADING

Mr John Newton

Your ref

Our ref    IAT/FOIA/51532

Date       2 March 2009

Direct line   (020) 7211 8801

Email         Ian.Bennett@oft.gsi.gov.uk

Dear Mr Newton

**REQUEST FOR COMPLAINT INFORMATION REGARDING MR VANCE MILLER TRADING AS 'KITCHENS'**

I refer to your letter of 2 January 2009 and in which you request details of the **"the nation-wide incidence of complaints against Kitchens and Vance Miller that came through Trading Standards"** for the period 1 January 2008 to 31 December 2008, and our subsequent correspondence.

As you have mentioned, the OFT's previous letter of 16 January 2008 (attached for ease of reference) supplied you with equivalent information for the period from July 2004 to 31 December 2007. This was in response to your request dated 18 December 2008.

As with your previous request, in view of Mr Miller's renewed permission dated 20 January 2009 to allow you to ask for and receive what amounts to his personal information, we are treating your current request as a subject access request under section 7 of the Data Protection Act 1998 (DPA).

In relation to numbers of complaints against Kitchens "made through Trading Standards", as advised in our previous letter the OFT does not, strictly speaking, hold such information. However I can confirm that a total of 97 complaints against Kitchens were received by Consumer Direct during the period 1 January 2008 to 31 December 2008.

I should stress that this figure only represents complaints against Kitchens, which appeared to cease trading towards the end of 2007. It does not include complaints against any other business that may have been carried on by Mr Miller during this period.

**Appeals procedure**

If you wish to complain about the way in which your request for information has been handled, you may seek an internal review by writing to:

INVESTOR IN PEOPLE

Office of Fair Trading
Fleetbank House
2-6 Salisbury Square
London EC4Y 8JJ
Switchboard: (020) 7211 8000
www.oft.gov.uk

The Internal Review Co-ordinator
Room GS/03
Office of Fair Trading
Fleetbank House
2-6 Salisbury Square
London
EC4Y 8JX

We will deal with your complaint within 25 working days of receipt or, if this is not possible, advise you of a date by which we expect to have completed a review of your complaint.

If you remain dissatisfied with the OFT's response you have the right to complain to:

The Information Commissioner
DPA Complaints Resolution
Information Commissioner's Office
Wycliffe House
Water Lane
Wilmslow
Cheshire
SX9 5AF

Your sincerely

Ian Bennett
Data Protection Act Coordinator
OFT Information Access Team

cc    Mr Vance Miller

Date: 2nd March 2009
Our ref: AE/PRO1/149
Your ref:

**Oldham**
Council

**Mr J Newton**

**Legal and Democratic Services**
Environment Group
Level 4 Civic Centre, West Street
Oldham, OL1 1UL

Tel: 0161 770 3019
Fax: 0161 770 3701

Dear Mr Newton

**FREEDOM OF INFORMATION ACT REQUEST**

I write with reference to your request under the Freedom of Information Act relating to the number of complaints received by the Council in relation to Mr Vance Miller and his company Kitchens based at Maple Mill, Cardwell Street, Oldham between 30 November 2007 and 30 November 2008. I have now received from you a signed letter of authority from Mr Miller consenting to the release of the information.

Between 30 November 2007 and 30 November 2008 the Council received 158 complaint records where Kitchen/Kitchens was named as the premises and 12 complaint records that named Kitchens Direct, Maple Mill and Maple Industries. During the same period there were a further 8 service requests regarding Kitchens.

A complaint is where someone is making a specific allegation and a service request is where someone wants advice or information about a subject, but is not making an allegation.

Yours sincerely

Alan Evans
Group Solicitor
Direct line: 0161 770 3019
Email: alan.evans@oldham.gov.uk

# Appendix 2
## *OFT Top Ten Complaints*

Visit the OFT webs ite
Press releases
9 January 2007
TOP TEN COMPLAINTS
Consumer Direct reveals top ten complaints in 2006.

Consumer Direct, the government's telephone and online advice service, received more complaints about second hand cars bought from independent dealers than for any other specific goods or services in 2006.

The figures released today show that Consumer Direct logged 37,594 cases about second hand vehicles bought from independent dealers, 3.9 per cent of the total 963,684 cases recorded in 2006.

Complaints about mobile phone service agreements came second with 24,799 cases, while complaints about TVs took the number three slot with 18,311 cases. The lowest number of registered complaints concerned trams, with only 5 cases logged.

Each case recorded by Consumer Direct is logged using one of 453 product or service codes, enabling the service to build a picture of the areas causing most concern to consumers. This and other data is then used to inform and focus the resources and work of Local Authority Trading
Standards Services and the Office of Fair Trading.

Although the results were fairly consistent across the country, there were some differences. The highest number of complaints to Consumer

Direct from callers in London concerned m service contracts, while leather furniture was the number one complaint in Scotland.

By sorting the 453 specific complaint codes into 66 general complaint categories, the top three complaint areas were home maintenance and improvements accounting for 7.7 per cent of cases, second hand cars at 6.6 per cent and telecommunications at 5.8 per cent.

In total, Consumer Direct took just over 1.5 million telephone calls and emails from consumers in 2006, up 79 per cent against the previous year, due in part to centres (in the North West, North East and the West Midlands) and a growing awareness of the service among the general public.

Christine Crvne. Director for Consumer Direct at the Office of Fair Trading said : ' In 2006, Consumer Direct successfully extended its operations to cover the whole of Great Britain. By offering more people access to the service , we have been able to gain greater intelligence about the main issues facing consumers.'

Consumer Direct provides information about consumer rights and advises callers on how to seek redress when things go wrong. The service is managed by the Office of Fair Trading and delivered in partnership with Local Authority Trading Standards Services.

http://www.consumerdirect.gov.    uk/news/press_ releases/national/2007/top_ten_compl... 16/07/2007

Consumer Direct - TOP TEN COMPLAINTS Page 3 of 4

People needing consumer advice can call 08454 040506 or visit the website at www.consumerdirect. govuk

Top Ten Complaints about specific goods and services in 2006

Category
No of cases
Percentage of total cases
Second hand cars purchased from independent dealers
37594 3.9
Mobile Phones (service agreements) 24799 2.6
TVs 18311 1.9
Other general building work 17503 1.8
Mobile Phones (hardware) 17115 1.8
Personal Goods and Services (Other) 15223 1.6
Car repairs and servicing from independent garages
14498 1.5
Upholstered furniture 14426 1.5
Fitted Kitchens - 12819, 1.3
Second hand cars purchased from franchise dealers
12641 1.3
Overall complaint trends in 2006
Category No of cases
Percentage Of total cases
Home maintenance and Improvements 74078 7.7
Second Hand Cars 59562 6.2
Telecommunications 55733 5.8
Furniture
Audio-visual
49641 5.2
38661 4.0
Large Domestic Appliances, 304245 3.2
Personal Computers, accessories, software and
services 26292 2.7
Clothing and clothing fabric 23995 2.5
http://www.Consumerdirect.gov.uk/news/press_
releases/national/2007/top_ten_compl... 16/07/2007

# Appendix 3
## *Vance Miller Police Interview Transcript*

Appendix 3

**OLDHAM**
Metropolitan Borough

### RECORD OF TAPE RECORDED INTERVIEW

| | | | | |
|---|---|---|---|---|
| Person Interviewed | Vance Miller | | Exhibit No. JC/1801605/TRANK | |
| Company Represented | | | Number of Pages | Six |
| Place of Interview | Chadderton Police Station | | Signature | |
| Date of Interview | 7th June 2007 | | | |
| Time Commenced | 11:12am | Time Concluded | 11:20 | |
| Duration of Interview | 8 mins | Tape Reference No (s) | 1801605 | |
| Interviewing Officer(s) | John Cassin, Nicola Orbison | | | |
| Other Person(s) Present | Alan Neal (Solicitor) | | | |

| Tape Counter Time | Person Speaking | Text |
|---|---|---|
| 0.10 | JC | This interview is being tape recorded and is being conducted at Chadderton Police Station. The date is the 7th June 2007 and the time by my watch is 11:12am. I am John Cassin, a Trading Standards Officer with Oldham Metropolitan Borough Council. The other officer present is - |
| | NO | Nicola Orbison, Senior Trading Standards Officer for Oldham. |
| | JC | Also present in this room is - |
| | AN | Alan Neal from Burton Copeland Solicitors of Manchester |
| | JC | Please could you state your full name and date of birth? |
| | VM | Vance Miller, 30/5/65 |
| | JC | And your home address please? |
| | VM | The Cemetery Lodgehouse, Ramsbottom |

*Kitchen Gangster?*

Record of Tape Recorded Interview of **Vance Miller**

| Tape Counter Time | Person Speaking | Text |
| --- | --- | --- |
| 0.50 | JC | At the conclusion of this interview I will give you a notice which explains what will happen to the tapes. Before we go any further I must caution you that: You do not have to say anything but it may harm your defence if you do not mention when questioned something which you later rely on in court. Anything you say may be given in evidence. Do you understand the caution? |
| | VM | Yes |
| | JC | Just so that I'm satisfied that you understand the caution I'll just explain it. You don't have to answer any of the questions that I'm going to ask today but if the matter does go to court and you decide to answer the questions at that stage, the court can make its own mind up why you chose not to answer the questions at the interview. If this case does go to court they can be told what you have said today. Do you understand that? |
| | VM | Yes |
| | JC | You have a legal representative with you today and are you happy to continue with this? |
| | VM | Yes |
| | JC | You've been arrested today so that questions can be put to you to determine the facts surrounding the offences of possessing dangerous quad bikes, in contravention of the General Product Safety Regulations, and also failing to undertake sample testing of the quad bikes and supplying a quad bike in contravention of a Suspension Notice issued to you on the 29th November 2006. Our role is to establish all the facts surrounding these offences and to fully investigate all the enquiries relating to the offence. As investigators we're open-minded to all the circumstances surrounding this investigation. This is now your opportunity to give your version of events on this tape recorded interview and I must remind you that you're under caution. |

LG25

99

tape\514

*280*

Continuation Page 3

Record of Tape Recorded Interview of **Vance Miller**

| Tape Counter Time | Person Speaking | Text |
|---|---|---|
| 2.32 | AN | Can I just intervene for a moment and say this before you get started with your questions. It's a point that I made to you earlier when you were carrying out disclosure and I have no complaint about the disclosure. What I do have a complaint about, and I made it clear to you at the time, was the fact that Mr Miller is here for an entirely different reason this morning, a reason with which you and your department are well familiar. There has been discussion between myself and members of your department concerning the issue which you're now dealing with and I must express my disappointment, considerable disappointment, at the fact that there's no indication in any of those recent conversations that I've had with your superiors that you were going to put these matters to my client this morning. I think that's capable of a certain conclusion and I'll say no more about it today, but I just wanted it to be a matter of record. |
| | JC | Right, that point's taken. |
| | VM | I'd also like to say at this point that you've mentioned there that you're open-minded into this investigation. Don't talk crap to me OK, you are not open-minded whatsoever. You are not here to investigate a reported crime, you're here to invent a crime aren't you, you're here to find a crime because you want my mill don't you, you want Maple Mill, because Oldham Council has been given a hundred and sixteen million pounds to spend on my mill. You've done deals with Park Cake Bakeries, you've done deals with Earl Mill, you've done deals with Belgrave Mill but you want my mill in the middle. I'm going to ask you a question, when you've answered my questions, yeah, I'm going to then answer your questions, OK. So what we're going to do is, we're going to swap question for question, OK. This is now my chance to interview you's because I suspect you's of conspiracy to steal my mill from me, yeah. I also suspect you for lying to the public, for lying to the police, lying to the newspapers, OK. So, I'm going to ask you now one simple question. If you answer |

LG25

100

tape\514

Record of Tape Recorded Interview of   Vance Miller

| Tape Counter Time | Person Speaking | Text |
| --- | --- | --- |
| 4.45 | | it, I'll then answer your questions. if you don't answer it, I will not answer any more of your questions, OK. Why was it that you've said to the media that I have fifty thousand complaints, that they're coming in at a hundred a week, when we made you prove under the Freedom of Information Act how many complaints I really had, you could only come up with seventy three. Explain yourselves. Over to you, you first. |
| | NO | You want me to explain that? |
| | VM | Yes please |
| | JC | Well that's not the matter that we're |
| | VM | Are you interfering, no it isn't the matter, nor is these quads the matter that we're here to discuss today either is it. The matter that we're here to discuss is the fact that I sell people wood and at the last minute I secretly swap it for chipboard. You are full of crap aren't you, you're just trying to invent a crime. You've had seven months of all my paperwork and you've made statements in the newspaper that you've got everybody in the office involved, everybody, the whole department is probing Vance Miller's affairs to find something. Well guess what, seven months later you've got nowt, nothing, zero. Now a private company would throw the towel in at that stage, they would say well seven months, the whole office has routed his affairs, we can't find anything, he obviously hasn't done anything. But oh no, not you lads, you double, you double the amount of officers looking for nothing don't you. Don't fuckin' start telling me, you prick, that you're fuckin' here and you're going to look at it with open fuckin' views and all that shit, you're full of fuckin' crap pal. Answer my fuckin' questions and I'll answer your questions, go on. |
| | JC | Well let's get back onto |
| | VM | Answer the fuckin' question. |

|0|

Continuation Page 5

Record of Tape Recorded Interview of **Vance Miller**

| Tape Counter Time | Person Speaking | Text |
|---|---|---|
| 6.40 | JC | We haven't made any statement |
| | VM | Fuck you prick, answer the question or I'm going out of this room now. |
| | JC | Right, if |
| | VM | Bye bye, lets go |
| | AN | You're under arrest. |
| | VM | Yeah, well I'm not staying in this fuckin' room, go and put me in my cell, I'm not answering any more of your questions. You are here to find a crime in what I say aren't you, you're going to take away all my words and you'll think there must be a crime somewhere in what he's said, lets find a crime somewhere. You're not interested in solving crimes, you're only interested in fuckin' making fuckin' crimes and charging me with them. You know that, you know that and we know that, yeah. Go and fuckin' nick somebody that's doing something fuckin' wrong, go and do your job. Why do you think you lost fuckin' thirty nine million pounds last year, Oldham Council. Why are you the 149th out of 150 worst managed fuckin' council in the fuckin' country. 'Cos you're bent, you're fuckin' crooks and I will expose you for being bent as well. I guarantee you pal, you will all go down for being fucking bent, I will expose Oldham Council and I will then bankrupt Oldham Council. You don't become 149th out of 150 worst managed fuckin' council by doing your job correctly, do you. I am the largest independent in the world at what I do. Don't you, the second worst at what you do, fuckin' start telling me how to run my business, you fuckin' half wits, you're half wits. Fuck your file, fuck your questions, I ain't answering any until you answer mine, go on, answer the question I asked, why did you lie to the tune of fuckin' fifty thousand down to seventy three, go on, why the big difference. |
| | JC | We're not here to answer your questions. |

LG25

102

tape\514

*283*

*Kitchen Gangster?*

Record of Tape Recorded Interview of **Vance Miller**

| Tape Counter Time | Person Speaking | Text |
|---|---|---|
| 8.45 | VM | Well are you not, well in that case I'm not here to answer yours, get me to my cell, let's go, give me a room please. Go and have a word with Tony fuckin' Allen, say Vance said he will answer all my questions but we've got to answer his first. Bye bye. |
| | JC | For the benefit of the tape Mr Miller is leaving the room and I'm switching off the tape recorder. |

LG25

103

tape\514

# Appendix 4
## *Alastair Cook Statement*

To whom it may concern

My name is Alastair Cook. I have recently noticed on the web and also in a number of newspaper articles a statement from Oldham Trading Standards referring to Vance Miller's appearance on BBC2 series, Notorious. In my view this is mentioned by Oldham Trading Standards in a manner and style designed to mislead the readers of these articles into believing that Notorious showed Vance Miller in a bad light, when it in fact shows quite the opposite.

To put you in the picture I would like to explain that in 2002 I was commissioned by the BBC to make a documentary about the business practices of Vance Miller. After reading many newspaper articles on Vance Miller, which cited thousands upon thousands of complaints to Trading Standards, I was convinced that I was going to uncover a scam on a huge scale. But after filming over a period of many months and having unrestricted access to all areas of the business I was convinced that Vance Miller was not operating a scam.

Vance Miller is an ambitious and driven businessman who has built up an enormous and successful company that employs thousands of people worldwide. If he was a conman then he's certainly not a good one, after all why would he need 800 staff in Britain and 2000 staff in China and operate from what is the largest mill complex in the north of Britain. Conmen (and I have filmed a few during my career) do not invest so heavily into their business. A conman would simply operate his scam from a small office somewhere. Why would they need all these staff and such a huge manufacturing capacity?

The press headlines surrounding Vance make good copy for journalists. He's labelled as a "Rogue Trader" or "A Conman" in every article. This label sticks and is passed from journalist to journalist but none of those writing the damning articles have ever met Vance or seen first hand his business. People always take as true what they read in the press but so often the papers print inaccuracies (often because they are just repeating what other papers have printed).

The series was called Notorious because the people in each of the films had notorious reputations. But that doesn't mean those reputations are valid. As a film maker I sought to discover for myself whether Vance's notorious reputation was accurate and I am convinced it is not. The film was titled "The Kitchen Gangster", to attract viewers and as a tongue-in-cheek jibe at all the bad press.

Vance is an unorthodox businessman. He favours tracksuits to suits. He calls a spade a spade. He doesn't't suffer fools. But he is extremely hard working and very sharp. He has the qualities needed to build a successful business. What Vance Miller has achieved is truly remarkable, building from nothing what is today the fourth largest kitchen company in Britain.

I have since made another documentary that features Vance, called Brits Get Rich in China (broadcast on Channel 4 in May 2007). I spent many weeks on the road with Vance in China watching him doing business. His schedule is exhausting, his operation vast and his knowledge of China second to none. That is why his business is so big – not because he rips customers of but because he has cracked China long before any of his rivals.

So you must ask yourself, why is Vance being persecuted in the press? In whose interests is it that he is put out of business? These are questions yet to be answered…. Maybe I will tackle them in my next documentary!

I would be happy to provide a copy of either the Notorious documentary – The Kitchen Gangster - or Brits Get Rich in China.

I hope this statement clears up any doubts you may have about Vance Miller. I thought that my documentaries would have done that but it seems that newspapers are still churning out the same misleading and lazy articles.

Yours sincerely,

Alastair Cook
Director of Notorious & Brits Get Rich in China.

## Appendix 5
### *Christine Statement*

My name is Christine and I'm the Executive Producer of a weekly talk show based in the U.S. that focuses on doing business in China.

I just finished watching Alastair Cook's documentary on Brits Get Rich In China and immediately set out on the web to do more research on Vance Miller.

After wading through quite a few interesting articles on the "Kitchen Gangster", I'm convinced that Mr. Miller is living and working in the wrong country. I say that because his business tactics and relentless pursuit of opportunity in China would render him nothing short of "rock star" status here in the U.S. business landscape.

I've done business in China. I know what it's like. Mr Miller truly "gets" China and how it works. If he were to apply his know-how to the U.S. market, it's over for Home Depot and Lowes here as well.

Christine
The China Business Network

# Appendix 6
## *GM Police Questions List*

Dear Clare,

The best I can do for a list of questions is as follows: -

The First Mill Raid, 29th November 2006

1. Press reports say up to 130 police raided Maple Mill. Another press report refers to 100 police in the raid. Yet another refers to 130 police and Trading Standards officers in the raid. Which is the correct number of police and do the figures of 100 or 130 include those that went to the houses of Miller and some of his staff that morning?

2. The press figures for police attendance, widely touted, do not appear to have been challenged by the police authorities, so, if correct, why were so many police needed to enter commercial premises not known to be used for any violent illegal purpose such as guns or drugs?

3. Press reports at the time indicate the raid was to help investigate possible fraudulent trading. Is this correct? If not, what was the purpose of the raid and its intensity?

4. Why was the raid on commercial premises conducted in such a way?

5. My research indicates that the police took a large amount of money from Maple Mill under the Proceeds Of Crime Act. The raid was approaching three years ago and I do not believe the money has yet been returned. I know that Miller is facing fraud charges in September but he has not yet (and may never be) convicted of any crime that seems to justify such action. At what point will the money be returned to him?

6. At the time of the raid on Maple Mill the Trading Standards authorities justified their action by issuing complaints figures against Miller and his company amounting, by one of their calculations, to over 5000 complaints a year and stated that around fifteen thousand people are thought to have been conned out of millions. Were the police aware before agreeing to the raid that in the twelve months prior to the raid the actual Trading Standards figures obtained through Freedom Of Information amounted to 73?

7. The Maple Mill raid started before dawn but a fair number of press and television journalists seem to have been present prior to the police arriving on site. Did the police give prior information to press and television?

The Second Mill Raid, Sunday 11th January 2009

1. My research indicates that around seventy police raided Maple Mill in this second raid. Why were so many officers needed when the first raid two years earlier met no form of aggressive resistance?

2. What was the purpose and justification of this second raid, since it was so similar to the first?

3. As in the first raid an amount of money was removed from the premises. According to staff at Maple Mill around £40,000 was removed without receipt.

4. According to staff at Maple Mill when a receipt was obtained a day or two later, the amount receipted was £10,000. Has a proper accounting been made to confirm the amount confiscated and what has happened to the money, whether £10,000 or any figure up to the £40,000 claimed as taken by Maple Mill staff?

5. Although this second raid took place over two days, with police returning on Monday 12th January, no press or television attended the actual raid and no reports seem to have appeared in the press following the raid. A request for information on why no publicity, after the blanket publicity of the previous raid met with the comment that such a report may prejudice later legal proceedings. If this is correct why did not the same attitude apply to press and television interest in the previous raid of November 2006?

6. My research indicates that apart from the cash taken in the first raid, the main evidence removed was invoices, delivery notes and computer records. It appears that the second raid garnered more or less the same paperwork and records. Does this indicate that the first raid failed to find the expected evidence of fraud so a second raid was necessary to have another go? This question was put to me in conversation with a local journalist who has reported on Miller for many years and it seems a fair point that may, at some time, need an answer. So I would put this as a reasonable question in an interview.

So, Claire, I reckon that this list of questions, if answered, should help give the police a say in what are, at present, two very one-sided Chapters on the raids.

I look forward to hearing from you as soon as you have put my request and questions list up for permission.

Best wishes

John

After exchange of a few further Emails during which I came no closer to an interview I sent a final message to Clare: -

You have not replied to my further interview request of a week ago so I guess I will never receive permission to speak to MEP regarding the Big Mill Raid. You may have noticed I placed a wrong date for the start of the Case again Vance Miller. I said it starts on 14th August when I should have said 14th September. In probably bringing our exchange of Emails on this subject to a close I make one final point. When we first had contact I said your request for a list of questions is difficult because the nature of an interview means it starts with a question then leads on from there. Your comment in your most recent Email that the Police are not the right ones to answer my questions because, "Both sets of raids were led by Oldham Trading Standards so they were in charge of the organisation and planning, as well as the media handling." brings up my question, "If that is the case, what did Oldham Trading Standards tell MEP to cause them such fear that over a hundred police were used in the first raid and about seventy police in the second raid?"

This question relates to my previous comment that the raid could have been conducted by half a dozen officers simply knocking on the door. The raids in both cases took place on ordinary commercial premises and private homes. The raids were massive in personnel and aggressive in nature. These are facts. The ordinary observer would ask what frightening information was told to the Police by Trading Standards to result in such response?

These comments appear in the book, now nearing completion and ready for publication the moment the Big Fraud Case ends and, as I say in the book, are one sided simply because no one from MEP will speak with me to give reasoned replies to reasonable questions.

I find it sad that the Police place themselves in a position to be criticised in such a way by lack of reasonable response and openness. Best wishes, John.

APW/KB

HH Judge Jonathan Foster QC

0161 954 7500

Minshull St. Crown Court,
Manchester M1 3FS
Sitting at Crown Sq

R v Vance Miller
Nicola Brodie
Sadiya Hussein
Alan Ford

T077927/97112

Delivered 12/1/10
11.40ᵃᵐ

## FINAL RULING

1. On Wednesday 23.12.09 I ruled that this case would go no further and gave brief reasons as follows;
    a. The prosecution will be stayed as an abuse of the process of the court in that
        i. The investigation was misconceived from the start
        ii. The assessment of the developing evidence was unsatisfactory
        iii. The volume of material compromised an over view of the case and the process of full and prompt disclosure
        iv. Such that there cannot be a fair trial and it would be unfair for these Ds to be tried further
    b. Further there is no case to answer on Cts 1 and 2; the proportion of complaints to sales is inconsistent with a concerted dishonest course of conduct.

    This ruling sets out my full findings and reasons. I say at the outset that this was an unusual case. The charge was conspiracy to defraud but there was no evidence of gain, nor any evidence of the turnover of the business or the proportion of fraudulent transactions. During the course of the trial attention changed from VM to the manner of OTS's investigation

## BACKGROUND

2. HISTORY – The Business; The prosecution allege that for a number of years VM had operated a variety of companies selling kitchens; the other D's were his trusted lieutenants. VM mainly operated from Maple Mill where the Kitchens were prepared or made. The companies, which were indistinguishable from VM, advertised in the press and through roadside advertisements. Dissatisfied customers complained about a variety of matters; the central allegation in the alleged conspiracy to defraud was the representation that the kitchens were made of real or solid wood with no chip board or the like, which they were not. There

I

were other alleged common features of paying the full price before delivery, rushed deliveries at inconvenient times, and difficulties getting any meaningful response out of the company or its complaint department. Some made the best of a bad job, others replaced their kitchens but got no recompense.

3. Personnel; The Prosecution case is that VM was the owner and driving force of the various businesses. The evidence alleges that he was at the centre of everything but when publicity was adverse he hid himself behind the names of others. NB lived with him and was closely involved in the business, particularly with the advertisements. SH was the manager of the business, knew the business' practises and was involved in the complaint handling. AF became a front for VM.

4. Stop Now Proceedings; In 2002 the OFT obtained Stop Now Orders in the M/c County Court restraining VM and others from selling goods which did not comply with description. In June 2003 HHJ Holman found VM in breach of those orders and sentenced him to 9 months imprisonment. The focus of the case was defects and misdescriptions generally, not specifically the real/solid wood issue which is the subject of this trial. 5 weeks later VM purged his contempt on giving undertakings that he would appoint management consultants to assist him with his business.

5. In early 2004 it was anticipated there would be a number of educational meetings between Oldham MBC Trading Standards Department (OTS) and VM and his staff. One such meeting took place on 19.01.04 and was summarised in a letter from OTS on 02.02.04 noting 19 points of discussion and the good progress made. There was a request for information about business names, to which VM did not appropriately respond. Thereafter there were telephone conversations about every three weeks between Daniel Moore (DM) of OTS and Kelly Jones on behalf of customer services at Maple Industries.

6. Over the next 2 years OTS kept a watching brief and liaised with OFT, ASA and other TS's (2 or 3 of whom brought TDA prosecutions) as they saw appropriate. OTS were the Home Authority and could have taken a more proactive role either by advice and assistance or if necessary enforcement. I had earlier been unimpressed by the "somewhat passive role" adopted by OTS as Home Authority. I was not convinced by DM's explanation that VM was perceived to be uncooperative. I find that DM was reasonably happy with this arrangement and did not perceive any great problem with VM's trading activities.

7. Summer 2006; After Easter Mr Allen (TA, Head of OTS) perceived an increase in complaints about Maple Mill. In June he began considering what should be done and by mid July had decided that the business should be investigated and the premises searched, hopefully in mid August. The concern was the description of high quality solid wood kitchens which were in fact low quality chip board, and a possible conspiracy to defraud involving the named Ds and Kelly Jones. In the event the "search" did not take place until the end of November.

8. RAID; On 29.11.06 Maple Mill, the main premises of the various businesses, was raided under a joint operation of OTS and GM Police. A total of over 130 people were deployed. The operation started with a briefing about 0300 and the raids started shortly after 0500. The targets were not only the Mill but the homes of the 4 defendants. The Police entered first to "secure" the premises, followed by TS officers who conducted the searches. An expert from FIRA was present but not adequately utilised and not called as a witness. There were teams of about 12 at each of the D's homes. A great deal of material was removed from the Mill including computers, the server, and 270,000 pages documents. Their return could not be described as speedy. TS issued a number of Press Releases explaining what had happened and what customers should do in the event of difficulty. In my view the press releases were likely to cause concern rather than reassure. During the course of argument, I used the phrases "heavy handed" and "overzealous" about the conduct of the raid. In the subsequent interviews VM and AF gave a prepared statements, SH set out her role in the business, and NB made no comment.

9. CHARGES;The Ds were not charged until 27.11.07; Vance Miller (VM), Sadiya Hussein (SH), Nicola Brodie (NB) and Alan Ford (AF) were charged with conspiracy to defraud between 2001 and 2006. VM and AF were later charged with 2 Statutory conspiracies between 2007and 2009. There were a further 10 substantive counts under the TDA 1968 which I quashed as out of time. The charges alleged the mis-selling of kitchens between 2001 and 2009. The central allegation was that the kitchens were described as being made of real or solid wood whereas they were made of laminate or chipboard.

10. Stop Now 07-08; In May 2007 OFT commenced further proceedings for breach of the Stop Now order. The proceedings were heard in May 08. The allegations did not concentrate on the wood issue. VM received a 9 month suspended sentence.

11. Quad Bike Prosecution; A floor of Maple Mill was found to contain a large quantity of Chinese Quad Bikes during the course of the Raid. This resulted in a Crown Court prosecution in December 08. The trial lasted about 10 days and was dismissed because of the inadequacy of the Prosecution (OTS) expert evidence.

12. Wang Raid Jan 09; From Febuary 2008 TA perceived that VM was continuing to trade in the same way as alleged in the previous conspiracy charges. A second raid was effected on 11.01.09. VM gave lengthy interviews alleging that that he was being persecuted by OTS and TA, and inviting OTS to visit his Mill.

13. Meeting Mar 09; Despite the above there was an exchange of correspondence between VM and OTS which resulted in a meeting on 06.03.09. VM recorded the meeting. TA's approach was in sharp contrast to his previous stance and ended with an approach to plea bargain.

3

14. This trial commenced 14.09.09. It started with 2 weeks argument on abuse of process during which I heard evidence from TA and DM. I delivered a short judgment on 28.09.09 and full reasons on 25.11.09. I then found TA's integrity not impugned. The arguments then centred on double jeopardy, OTS following its own procedures and the joinder of the other Ds to justify conspiracy. The arguments are now wider and the arguments on wrongful joinder of the other Ds take on a slightly different complexion in the light of my reasons for saying no case to answer on Cts 1 + 2

15. Approach to Abuse and no case to answer;
    a. The burden is on the D to establish abuse of process. The standard of proof is the balance of probability. In this process the Judge is the finder of facts.
    b. No case to answer; the law is well understood from R v Galbraith 1981 73 CAR 124 CCA, A 4-294. Where the judge concludes that the prosecution evidence, taken at its highest, is such that a jury, properly directed, could not properly convict, it is his duty, on a submission being made, to stop the case.
    c. There are 4 Ds, but all revolve around VM. If the case fails against him, it fails against them all

16. Evidence; I heard evidence before the jury over 13 weeks. In broad terms it encompassed evidence from dissatisfied customers, Advertisers, Salesmen, ASA, OFT, and OTS from TA, KR, and DM. I have summarised the factual background above. My factual findings on abuse are evident from the analysis which follows.

THE INVESTIGATION

17. TA said he saw indications of rising complaints after Easter 2006. By June he considered whether he ought to investigate further. On 21.07.06 he sent an email to OFT and GMP proposing a target profile and a raid in mid August. On 24.07.06 he set out his views to OFT at a meeting in London, which was minuted by Emma Hodgson of OFT. Its contents are not disputed.

18. The decision to investigate was not based on any reliable material;
    a. There was no discernible increase in complaints by Easter 06. The figures from the fortnightly tactical assessments were reasonably steady. TA conceded that they were not then wholly reliable and it is therefore difficult to rely on any trend.
    b. VM kitchen complaints were not separated from the general data until 18.07.09, and even then did not identify how many related to wood
    c. DM saw no apparent rise in complaints
    d. TA's rationale for his belief in increased complaints changed during his evidence: He ultimately relied on a graph on the draft target profile but dated 22.08.06. This was not disclosed until 17.12.09 towards the end of

4

his evidence. He then said he saw earlier drafts, but they cannot have been earlier than sometime after 21.07.06. No such earlier drafts were ever produced.

e. Putting back the date of his belief in increased complaints and the decision to raid justified his changed rationale but contradicted his earlier evidence about when he decided to investigate.

f. I find this late disclosure particularly unfortunate given the known concern about the investigation and particularly my ruling on 28.09.09 which TA considered.

19. I am concerned there may have been other reasons for the decision to investigate;
   a. 3 emails passed between TA and OFT on 17,18 and 21 July 06.
   b. On 17.07.06 TA spoke of significant media and local member interest on VM and was considering alternative and more rapid tactics than further contempt proceedings.
   c. On 18.07.06 (read full email) he suggested seizing the kitchens and the manufacturing equipment as evidence of a cheat. "with no equipment and no kitchens, might this have the effect of ceasing his operations more directly than stop now powers have achieved" This email only came to light through disclosure from the OFT in late Nov 06. Presumably it would have been on TA's computer but this was unfortunately recycled in 2007.
   d. On 21.07.06 he wrote "it is plain from our assessment that Mr Miller and his staff are engaged in a conspiracy to defraud the general public through their trading operations. This level of complaints is unprecedented even for Mr Miller...I have therefore tasked officers to generate a target profile for Mr Miller and plan a multi-agency operation in mid August...in the past Mr miller has exhibited violence towards law enforcement officers...we may need tactical aid...we have a large array of statements"
   e. On 24.07.06 TA met senior officers of the OFT in London. There are 5 pages of minutes prepared by Emma Hodgson from OFT litigation department. Again these minutes were only disclosed in late Nov. TA said he had no preparatory notes for the meeting, and no notes of the meeting. I find the lack of preparatory notes surprising since Ms Hodgsons minute reveals an extremely well prepared presentation.
   f. I will not attempt to summarise the meeting. I will refer to further extracts in my assessment of TA. It ends "the options available to OTS are (1) put him out of business by default by seizing all his assets (it may also be possible to just disable his machinery); and (2) put him out of business by injunction (I am not sure what this means)". TA contemplated a charge of conspiracy to defraud with a possible sentence of 4-6 yrs. His conception of a raid was clearly fairly well advanced.
   g. During the abuse hearing in September TA repeatedly said that it was not his intention to close the business down, although he acknowledged that was a possible consequence of the raid. During his evidence before the

5

jury in December he conceded that it was his desire to close the business down. "I'd like to close the business down right to this day". In the light of the recent disclosure from the OFT, the concession was difficult to avoid, but nevertheless revealed an alarming inconsistency and contradiction in his evidence.

20. Appointment of Kirsty Robinson as Senior Investigating Officer
    a. In the summer of 2006 KR had 4 yrs experience working with TS following a degree. She had just been appointed a senior TS officer. She had no experience of an operation of this nature or size. I do not doubt her integrity or ability but she was not sufficiently experienced for this role.
    b. DM had a similar background. He had had the day to day dealings with Maple Mill since early 2004 when he must have been in his mid 20's at most. I repeat my comment in my earlier judgment that he was asked to shoulder responsibility beyond his experience.
    c. TA rightly accepted responsibility for the operation and the prosecution as the senior man. There were weekly meetings between TA, KR and DM, but operation was effectively run by KR and DM. TA did not know a lot of the detail. For instance he did not know the contents of VM's interviews after the Jan 09 raid.
    d. The result was that the decision making structure was largely ineffective.
    e. The manner of KR appointment is also unusual. She is recorded as being SIO from July06. KR says ,and I accept, that she did not know of her role until her return from leave in mid November. She was not part of planning meetings with GMP in September as asserted by TA in evidence.

21. Execution of Raid
    a. I have described the Raid in paragraph 8 above. Having considered the whole of the evidence phrases such as heavy handed and overzealous do not sufficiently describe the operation. I find it disproportionate and oppressive.
    b. Furthermore it singularly failed to achieve its objective. The briefing pack contained a page titled key items to look for. These included samples. TA in evidence said that he purpose of the raid was to see what was going in and out of the Mill. An expert on wood from FIRA was present but misused. No inventory of what was in the Mill was taken
    c. Instead 270000 pages of documents were uplifted. The task of sifting this volume of material was daunting. It was beyond the resources of OTS, as illustrated in para 22 below. Furthermore although VM's was plainly a paper business, his working documents were returned electronically over a number of months.

22. Use of the material recovered in the raid;

a. Prior to the raid TA did not believe there was any natural wood in the mill. He said he still did not think there was after the 2$^{nd}$ raid in January 09. KR and DM held similar views. This was an important issue because if there was no wood the adverts were manifestly false. Conversely if there were substantial quantities of natural wood, then E/ees, particularly the co Ds, could argue that they believed the adverts to be true.

b. Despite the obvious importance of the issue no simple inventory was ever prepared detailing what was in the Mill. TA asserted that the information could be derived from the exhibits, but nobody attempted to do so, no doubt because it was an impossible task.

c. Moreover there were a number of exhibits, particularly SHs diary, invoices for wood, and Maple News which indicated there were substantial quantities of natural wood going in and out of the Mill. These documents were never analysed, indeed the investigation team were not aware of the content of most of them. Thus there was no return visit to ascertain the truth of the situation, thus depriving the defence of a proper opportunity to establish their case.

d. I have already commented that there is no evidence of turnover either by value or volume of sales. There was sufficient information in the recovered material to make some estimate of these matters and in any event other lines of enquiry to ascertain the position, eg VAT or income tax returns, or bank A/cs. It would similarly have been useful to have some idea of the proportion of trade to retail sales.

e. There were other items of importance to the overall complexion of the case, eg the DHL invoices (according to the defence evidencing prompt replacement of damaged items etc) which were marked irrelevant and returned to VM, and the rule book, a rudimentary attempt of instructions to Salesmen, customer services etc.

f. I conclude there was no effective consideration let alone analysis of the material recovered. This prevented OTS from taking an overview of the case and discharge their duties of proper and full disclosure.
(inj)

23. Evidence of customers
a. Prior to the raid only one customer, Mr Wheatley, had been interviewed. This does not sit easily with TA's email of 21.07.06 that OTS had a large array of statements. In fact OFT had some completed Questionaires and OTS had flare records, which was a computer record of customer complaints.

b. Mr Wheatley was an unfortunate choice because during the course of his evidence, on being confronted by a tape recording, he conceded that he had attempted to blackmail VM. In any event his story required some scrutiny because the price was many times higher than any other sale, and involved a doubling in price by the delivery driver that Mr Wheatley was able to pay on demand in cash.

7

c. During the course of the trial the individual complainant customers have been tested against their first complaints and tape recorded interviews given to OTS for the preparation of a witness statement. Counsel, coordinated by Miss Roberts have produced a schedule attempting to analyse the nature of the complaints. It is right to note that wood was not always their first complaint, and in some cases was not part of their complaint until contact with TS. In other cases there have been replacements or some form of satisfaction, in others a motivation for gain, and in others the possibility of genuine mistake or misunderstanding. However there remain a core of complainants who could be properly described as being misled by the advertisements

d. Mr Watson QC prepared an analysis of the proportion of complaints to Sales. It was based on some assumptions, but TA (and I) accept it as a reasonable exercise. On the basis that all the complaints are well founded, there are .29% of wood complaints to total sales, and less than 4% of total complaints to sales. The proportions may well be less if misunderstanding etc is taken into account

e. Regrettably there are no comparative figures for other Kitchen companies, but Counsel and witnesses have proceeded on the basis that kitchens attract a high level of complaints.

f. I am also mindful of the adverse press coverage. In my view that was caused in large part by OTS's own Press releases which would hardly have reassured consumers. Such press coverage would be capable of contaminating the approach of consumers.

24. Evidence of Salesmen; The prosecution called 3 ex-salesmen, Walters Rook and Manning. 2 spoke of rudimentary training, one of no training. There was no suggestion of any attempt to encourage them to misrepresent the products; rather they seemed concerned to ensure the customer knew what he was getting, alongside getting a sale! The rule book instructed Salesmen not to use the term solid wood. Adverts for Salesmen discouraged pressure salesmen from applying. Whilst the fraud could be perpetrated without the salesmen, it would be difficult to operate without some tacit understanding with them. If anything they were good witnesses for the defence.

25. Expert evidence; OTS retained Mrs Sue Calver from FIRA to attend at the raid. She played little useful part at that stage. Later she examined some of the complainants kitchens. She was not called as a witness. I saw her report which had points for both sides. Not surprisingly the Defence repeatedly tried to get the favourable parts before the Jury. They were largely unsuccessful. I do not think an expert was necessary in this case, although a review of the contents of the Mill would have been helpful. Nevertheless it was unhelpful to the prosecution that the jury knew they had used an expert but not called her.

8

26. Disclosure; The issue of the basis for the belief that there were increasing complaints was evident from the very start of the case and highlighted in my judgment of 28.09.09. Despite this

    a.  The fortnightly tactical assessments were not produced until some time in November 09. Yearly or quarterly summaries had been annexed to a statement from TA in Aug 09. Some of the detail form the basis of a graph referred to in the Stop Now proceedings in May 08, but that detail was not disclosed in these proceedings until Nov09.

    b.  The final Target profile was listed in the sensitive schedule, and the draft not ~~specifically~~ listed at all.

    c.  The target profile was disclosed on 29.11.09 but the draft and 3 files of material from Sally Jones the tactical analyst were not disclosed until 17.12.09, the penultimate day of evidence. The files were cryptically described in the list of unused in Wang, and against the volume of material it is unsurprising they were missed. I have seen a list of the contents of the files but not the files themselves. I accept GG that it potentially contains highly relevant material which may well have been used in xx, and affected the defences approach to the case. VM made similar arguments.

    d.  GG further told the court that further material from Consumer Direct was disclosed at the same time as the files. It would have been material to xx TA. GG says this engenders no confidence in the disclosure regime, and queries whether in those circumstances there can be a fair trial.

    e.  Despite lack of evidence of the Nov 06 raid, a police video was recently discovered in TA's cupboard

    f.  The recycling of TA's computer in 2007. I was told on the last day of submissions that it would be an admitted fact that TA had his computer routinely recycled in the summer of 2007. No doubt that explains why some of the emails only came to light through OFT disclosure. A computer is the equivalent of a filing cabinet. I know not what was on the computer. However I regard it as extraordinary that it should not have been retained as potentially relevant to this case.

27. Failure to follow regulatory procedures and OTS's own policies;

    a.  OMBC's Trading Standards and Licensing Department published their policy on 29.11.06. It was common ground that the document incorporated past policies and was effective at the material times. It reflected the Enforcement Concordat 2003 to which OMBC were a signatory. It describes procedural options ranging from verbal advice through to prosecution. It sets out 4 situations when prosecution may be justified and 3 tests, evidential, public interest and alternative resolution, which must be satisfied. It states that the availability of alternative resolution does not necessarily preclude cases being reported for enforcement action where the case is serious. It envisages a degree of discretion and is essentially directory rather than mandatory.

9.

    b. I repeat my earlier judgment that the decision to prosecute rather than seek some alternative resolution would not normally amount to an abuse. However it is a factor in the overall picture and must be set against
        i. The meeting on 06.03.09
        ii. VM requests to DM or TA to visit the Mill in September 2005 (ASA ruling), August 2006 (Granite complaint), October 2006 (when VM learnt of the raid) and January 09 during Interview.

28. Inability to look at the strength of their case. Breach of CPIA Code 3.5. The Investigator should pursue all reasonable lines of inquiry, whether these point towards or away from the suspect. In evidence TA said that the purpose of the raid was to obtain evidence to support his hypothesis. I do not think the matters set out above constitute the model objective approach

29. Wang Raid – 11.01.09. By Febuary 08 TA perceived that VM was continuing to trade as before. Another Raid therefore took place on 11.01.09.
    a. It is instructive to put the timing in context. This was 14 months after the Nov 07 charges, 8 months after suspended sentence in the May 08 Stop Now proceedings, and less than a month after the failed Quad bike trial.
    b. Whilst I accept that the raid was not oppressive in the same way as the Nov 06 raid, many of the same mistakes were made again
        i. No witness statements were taken prior to the raid
        ii. Whilst it was the intention to video the Mills floor by floor, the batteries on the 3 cameras ran out, after only one floor. No one thereafter continued a review making a comprehensive note of the contents of each floor, Yet again therefore there was no inventory.
        iii. No carcases were removed to illustrate the nature of the products
    c. VM was interviewed by DI Mayer who was not the SIO, and the charging decision taken by DS Glymond who had billed for only 77hrs work. TA did not read the interviews, nor was he told of their content, and would have charged in any event – with no investigation of numerous substantive matters raised therein.
    d. RART were present in relation to asset recovery. TA said OTS did not apply for details of VM's various bank a/cs, but he expected RART did. He did not know consequences. I found this a most disengenuous answer. TA knew that VM disqualified as Director, and therefore had to trade in his own name. This would inevitably make banking difficult. A further enquiry from RART would make it even more difficult to trade.
    e. Bail; Following the raid VM was held in custody until a bail application was made before me on 06.02.09. TA was present at Court. Bail was opposed on the grounds of the risk of further offences. I held that the earlier offences had not yet been proved and that the appropriate way to prevent further offences was through the Stop Now order. It would have been very difficult to trade from prison.

10

30. Meeting 06.03.09; After 5 years of virtually no contact with VM, OTS in the form of TA agreed to meet to see whether they could improve his business practices. It was in sharp contrast to his previous stance and his opposition to Bail a month earlier. It sits uneasily with his evidence that he would still like the business closed down, and his report to the OFT in April 09 that there was evidence that VM in breach of the Business names Act. Despite TA opposition to VMs Tape recording of the meeting (as to which I see nothing illegal), it was a good thing he did because the AG Guidelines require a tape recording for a plea bargain with an unrepresented D.

31. Assessment of TA;

   a. I previously found TA did not act from any improper motive and did not intend to close the business down; his integrity was not impugned.
   b. DW for NB now asserts that TA motivated by not just the prospect of closing the Mill down, but also by a lengthy sentence for conspiracy to defraud, thus necessitating (falsely) joining co-conspirators
   c. GG for SH asserts an ill motivated determined attempt to drive VM out of business using whatever means available.
   d. JG for AF, and VM make similar requests.
   e. This is not a trial of TA. But since these allegations are central to the defence submissions, and Mala Fides is a ground for Abuse, I do not think I can avoid addressing the issue

32. Unsatisfactory elements of TA's evidence;

   a. The assertion that there was an a basis for his belief in increased complaints
   b. Misrepresentations to the OFT at the meeting 24.07.06
   c. The contrast in his evidence between September and December 06
   d. The opposition to Bail in Febuary 09 and the meeting on 06.03.09
   e. Recycling of his computer
   f. As a matter of impression I did not find TA a dishonest witness, nor a person who was deliberately trying to manipulate his position for an improper purpose. However I have concluded that his initial desire to close the business down coloured his thinking thereafter. It led him to loose his objectivity so that he did not give a fair and balanced approach to the issues and the evidence in the case. Regrettably I find myself unable to rely on his evidence.

33. LAW ON ABUSE

n

Mr Gozem QC and Mr Mahmood have set out the principles in which a court can stay proceedings as an abuse of its process. Mr Field QC for the prosecution and counsel for the other Ds agree that it is a proper exposition of the law. In support I have been provided with a bundle of authorities.

a. The starting point is Connelly v DPP 1964 AC 1254 HL and DPP v Humphrys 1977 AC 1 HL ( see Archbold 4-48) from which it can be stated that the court will intervene where it concludes that a D cannot receive a fair trial and /or it would be unfair for a D to be tried.

b. Later cases have explained that the doctrine is capable of extending to manipulation or misuse of the process of the court, and unfairness by oppression and executive abuse, and delay.

c. Lord Scott in R v Crown Court at Leeds ex p Wardle 2002 1 AC 754 at para 155 neatly summarised the position "..It involves the use of court process for a purpose other than that for which the purpose in question was intended".

d. It does not necessarily require dishonesty mala fides or prejudice to the D

e. The categories of Abuse are not closed, but the power must be exercised judicially.

34. THE FACTS OF THE CASE IN RELATION TO ABUSE;

a. In Sept I did not consider the facts amounted to an abuse; I concluded that OTS's decisions should not be viewed with the benefit of hindsight and were made in good faith. The evidence has changed and I set out my findings below

b. The investigation was flawed from the start by TA's unsubstantiated belief that complaints were increasing and VM's businesses should be closed down

c. That belief continued throughout the investigation and compromised his objectivity

d. The Raid was oppressive

e. OTS failed to analyse the material available to them

f. Disclosure was late and incomplete compromising the integrity of the prosecution and depriving the defence the opportunity to consider the overall complexion of the evidence against them

g. The whole process was unfair to VM, his business and the CoDs who in my opinion were wrongly joined in these charges.

h. On the balance of probabilities the defence have established that they cannot receive a fair trial and that it would be unfair to try them further. The process is an abuse of the procedures of the court. I stay these proceedings.

NO CASE TO ANSWER

35. Counts 1 and 2 – Conspiracy to defraud by misrepresentations about wood;

12

    a.  OTS never attempted to analyse the proportion of complaints to sales about the nature of the wood. In the event it turned out to be very small. This is a poor start to establish a fraud.

    b.  The hallmarks of a conspiracy to defraud are gain and some indication of concerted dishonest action between the conspirators. There is no convincing evidence of either.

    c.  NB, SH, and AF have hardly featured in the case save for performing their roles within the business. Knowledge of the business is a far step from dishonest agreement.

    d.  The fact finding process is a matter for the Jury. They are entitled to draw inferences on the overall complexion of the evidence. This includes the possibility, as suggested by TA to VM on 06.03.09, that the complaints arose from incompetence rather than dishonesty.

    e.  I acknowledge Mr Field QC's argument that risk of prejudice to the rights of consumers could be proved without any evidence, but this denies the fact that the jury have heard evidence and must make their decision on that evidence.

    f.  I have made factual findings on abuse many of which impinge on the strength or weakness of the case. The Jury may or may not agree with those conclusions, but they illustrate the dilemmas with which they will have to grapple.

    g.  In my judgment a jury could not properly convict these Ds on these charges. Had I not stayed the prosecution for abuse, I would have withdrawn these counts from their consideration.

36. Count 3 – Conspiracy to defraud by misuse of the Business Names Act. This count is very different because the ingredients of the offence are essentially admitted. I would not withdraw this count from the Jury. However Mr Field QC realistically acknowledges that it could hardly stand alone.

37. Comment; Some may think that this trial has been a waste of time, money and emotional commitment. I consider that the trial process has been vindicated. It was only by the examination of the detail that the facts emerged. As I said in my brief reasons before Xmas, the investigation was misconceived from the start and OTS were overwhelmed by the volume of material they had recovered. In those circumstances it was unsurprising that the process of disclosure was inadequate. Whatever Mr Miller may have done, and I make no adverse aspertions, we shall never know.

38. I am extremely grateful the Jury for their patience during this long trial. The trial could not have gone ahead and these conclusions emerged without their part. I hope they respect my decision and the legal process by which it was reached. You are discharged from further Jury Service for the rest of your lives.

39. Finally I would like to thank Counsel and Mr Miller for their help during this long case. Mr Miller represented himself which posed particular problems for the

13